MW01254547

## STRAIGHT FROM THE

# HORSLEY'S

## MOUTH

*Michelle Horsley*

<u>This book would not have been possible without the generous help of family and friends.</u>

*Thank you -*

*... to my amazing cousin, Heather McClenahan Deyo, for all of her time and talents in helping with the cover design.*

*... to my uncle, Jon Clenahan, for drawing a horse which would aptly portray the silliness in many of these stories.*

*... to my life-long friends, especially Amy Adams, for helping to jog my memory.*

*... to my dear friend, Sadiq, whose professional help throughout the tedious process of printing a book has made this idea a reality.*

*... to all the coffee shops (The Beehive, 21st Street Coffee, Crazy Mocha, Espresso a Mano) where this book has been written and to all the baristas that now know me by name.*

*Well.*
*The printer malfunctioned again.*


*Love,*
*Michelle*

# TABLE OF CONTENTS

# STRAIGHT FROM THE

# HORSLEY'S

## MOUTH

# Preface

I should make one thing absolutely clear before we begin. This is by no means a comprehensive collection of everything that happened. There are so many stories which I have chosen to omit and ones I cannot remember well enough to tell. I have used many resources to try to put the pieces together of when and how things happened, but life is long and history is rich. There can be no complete retelling.

It's safe to say that many of humankind's greatest experiences have been a result of mere curiosity - the calling of adventure and desire to see what lies on the other side of the fence. It's not unreasonable to assume that many of our own adventures as a family have been for this same reason. We often yearn for something new, but how often do we actually seek it? How often to we let the comforts of our routines overpower our thirst for the unknown?

I'm twenty-three years old now, and although college and travels have caused my family to be apart, this past year is really the first year we have all gone our separate ways.

So many little things in the past year - even the most mundane things - have sparked the greatest memories of times we shared as a family. They say it's unhealthy to dwell on the past - a saying with which I completely agree - but this is something altogether different. This is my own way of coming to terms with the magic that was our past. I don't ever want these stories to get lost through generations, so this is my way of keeping them, immortalizing them. It has been quite the journey with so many stories.

Here are some of them.

# Chapter 1: The Early Years

As the story goes, my mom and dad fell in love, got engaged on a mountain in Hawaii, and married in Chicago in the year 1988. They wanted a clean slate on which to start their lives together so they moved to St. Petersburg, Florida and after looking at many houses, they ultimately bought the very first one they visited. This house on Meadowlawn Drive would become our "home base," so to say, for many decades to follow. There was a little park with a lake 3 blocks away called Meadowlawn Park, but even though they never again saw an alligator in the lake after that first visit, we have called it Alligator Lake ever since.

I was born in 1990 and, even though my parents weren't necessarily trying to have a child, they were ready. I was born in 1990 in my own bedroom. My parents chose to have a home birth and although the dog, Tina, proved to be a distraction throughout the long night, everything went as planned without any complications. My brother, Jason, was born in the living room two and a half years later. Mom and dad put up wooden storks outside of the property, announcing our births.

During that time, mom and dad were into their final years doing wedding gigs. My dad could do both the ceremony as the organist and the following reception as a band leader. He collaborated with area musicians to make up Ray Horsley Orchestras. My mother was one of the first to buy a videocamera, which in those days was a gigantic hunk of a contraption which you'd have to slug over your shoulder. The two of them were in high demand and had converted the living room into something of a studio to produce demo tapes and the like.

As babies, Jason and I had very different oral fixations. Like many babies, I was obsessed with sucking my thumb. I did, however, have a very unique demand that went along with the thumb-sucking. I absolutely had to have a single strand of hair wrapped around my thumb as well. My poor mother was forced to frequently yank out hairs from her own head so that I would be satisfied.

Jason, however, was fascinated with pacifiers. There must've been pacifiers in every room of the house and we would continue to find them even years later, hidden under couches or behind dressers. Jason developed a level of pacifier twirling proficiency which was unparalleled. He could flip it upside-down with one flick of the tongue. Sometimes dad would challenge adults to try it and it always left them astounded.

One of my dad's favorite memories was possibly the first time he heard me laugh. I was just this squirmy, helpless little thing of a person who wasn't yet capable of anything other than flailing in place. One day, I was on my back in the living when Tina, the dog, made the unfortunate mistake of walking within my reachable vicinity. I extended my arm and grabbed one of her hind legs. The poor old dog pulled back, instinctively, and I just kept tugging obnoxiously, giggling all the while. The dog quickly learned her lesson, much to the entertainment of my father and me.

In my early childhood, dad and I went on many great outings. A little trip to the library, for example, would quickly escalate into a bigger trip to a bookstore downtown and inevitably a whole afternoon of adventures around

town. Dad also started taking me to the symphony when I was very young. Every year for Christmas we saw Tchaikovsky's *The Nutcracker*. This was very important.

Naturally, Jason was very, very young during these adventures and therefore usually stayed home with mom. Dad's solution was to make a promise because of the age difference between Jason and me. Dad promised to make up this time to him many, many years later during the period in which I would have left home and Jason would still be there. And so it was.

There are many funny little stories from the times dad and I shared during these years. There was the time when dad surprised me with a trip to Disney, only to surrender all decisions to me once we entered the park. Like most very young children, I had no concept of waiting or lines or money. Sometimes, upon finally reaching the end of a 40-minute wait for a particular ride, I would suddenly just walk away and decide I would rather do something completely different. Instead of trying to talk sense into me, dad simply went along with the nonsense. Ultimately, we came across a little pond nestled in between various attractions. After all the fuss of calling off work, driving to Orlando, buying the expensive tickets, and standing around in lines for all these incredible attractions, ultimately all I wanted to do was feed the ducks. We could've easily walked 3 blocks from home to do the very same thing.

There was also the time when we were out on some excursion and dad was casually asked whether or not he had helped dress me that morning. It's important to note that dad took pride in these first parental achievements of taking me out to explore at a young age. Confidently he responded, "Why yes, I most certainly did!", to which he was shockingly informed that my dress was on backwards. Little moments like these still make us giggle.

Jason and I attended kindergarten at Lutheran Church of the Cross School (LCC), where we were taught by a sweet lady named Linda Pappas. I became especially close with a crazy girl name Elizabeth Spitzer. Mostly we played games and made crafts and attended the annual pumpkin patch. There was nap time everyday which involved laying out on towels in a multipurpose room. I was always too excitable to fall asleep. I remember the turkey painting we made for Thanksgiving by outlining our handprints. I'm sure we did tons of Christmas ornaments and the like as well. Mom kept all of our "art".

During these very early years, dad was also very interested in flying. He went downtown to the flying club frequently and even purchased his own Grumman Cheetah. Very briefly, mom and dad even had ideas of buying a

house which had a landing strip by it. Dad didn't have a license which allowed him to fly above a certain altitude, but he still was able to make many big trips to the Gulf of Mexico or to the Atlantic side of the state. I think they actually made it to the Keys once to go scuba diving. When I was a baby, they took me up in it a couple times. I would be perfectly fine while I was blissfully unaware of what was going on. However, as soon as I looked out the window, I would start crying and screaming uncontrollably. They quickly learned that this was not a good combination.

One day, however, dad's flying instructor, Johnny Mott, a man who seemed larger than life, died tragically in a plane crash just a few miles away from the flight school. Dad was very shaken by this and spent the next few days in the flight club playing "When Johnny Comes Marching Home" on the grand piano in the lobby. With a baby girl and another child on the way, he had the sudden realization that it was just not worth the risk. He sold his plane shortly after.

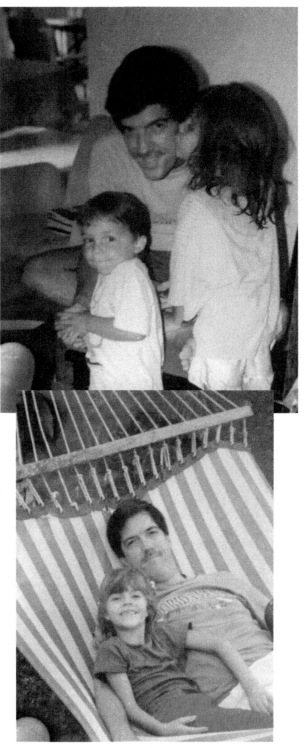

# Chapter 2:
## Homeschooling and Activities

Music was always playing in our house. I remember jumping on the couch and swinging around the legs of the grand piano while dad played Brahms' *Hungarian Dance #5*. I remember tracing my fingers through the ornate ridges on the sides of the Chickering. I remember the endless excitement from the long and tedious crescendo and feverish climax in Liszt's Rhapsody #23 in C-sharp minor. One day, while I was listening to dad play the piano, he turned to me and asked, "Would you like to be able to do this too?" to which I nodded, "yes". Piano lessons started when we were 5 years old. That's how it all began, I suppose. We had lessons every night, with very few exceptions, from 7-8pm, for over a decade.

The Jocelyn family lived directly across the street from us and had children of similar ages. Aaron, the youngest, was born a day before I was and we became the closest of childhood friends. The two of us had wild imaginations and would create entire kingdoms of which we were the rulers. We staged plays and tea parties with puppets and stuffed animals, which were naturally treated as if they were always real. When Jason was older, he joined in the friendship and the three of us spent countless hours goofing off after school.

Summers were spent splashing around in the pool, listening to music, and reading stories. I remember dad joking around that he could show us the pool's "underwear" by propelling himself off one of the walls and therefore causing a huge ripple of white in his path. We also regularly played games of "down n' back" which, quite simply, was just a race that involved swimming down to one end and then back.

Although the Jocelyn family had a very different style of parenting than us, we all got along swimmingly. Aaron had a military dad who wasn't too keen on the idea of him dressing up with me like fairy princesses, but we were kids and it was all very innocent. It seems like it was just simpler back then.

It's fair to say that Jason and I were, in a sense, home-schooled since the very beginning. Mom carefully researched the best, award-winning novels for children and every night we would snuggle up and listen to dad read to us. Whether or not we realized it at the time, I think that many of the themes from the books we were read reemerged in our lives later as important concepts or desires. Books like *The Boxcar Children Series* sparked a desire for travel and independence. *The Hatchet* instilled messages of resourcefulness and courage. We must have read over a hundred books during these years.

We also were obsessed with creative toys. Jason was constantly building the most elaborate creations with Legos. Naturally, you had to purchase the kits which came with specific pieces and instructions to make a certain design. Jason, however, would notoriously throw out the instructions and build his own design from his imagination. Along the same lines, we played with Kinex and Lincoln Logs, which were also very popular at the time.

After kindergarten, when it came time to choose a school for Jason and me, mom and dad had a hard time finding a good program in our area, so they chose to try homeschooling instead. This was really not such a new idea for them, since dad was already teaching us music every night. It was, however, a budding trend for the time. Mom joined PPEA (Pinellas Parent Educator's Association)

and got involved in the community. Through that organization, we met tons of other families, including the Terrys, the Simpsons, and the Grangers.

The homeschoolers also organized a weekly science class of sorts at North Branch Public Library with a strange man named Doug Skull. Mr. Skull had an obsessive love for animals and, because of a science educator's license, was allowed by the state to keep exotic animals in his house. Every week, he would drag a huge tupperware container through the entrance of the children's non-fiction section of the library - much to the librarians' horror - and unleash a snapping turtle, for example, in one of the meeting rooms. Sometimes we would meet outside the library in the adjacent Fossil Park. I remember one day he convinced us that fried ants were edible by hosting a cookout for everyone to try them. Doug Skull loved the kids and the kids loved him. There was never a dull moment in his classes.

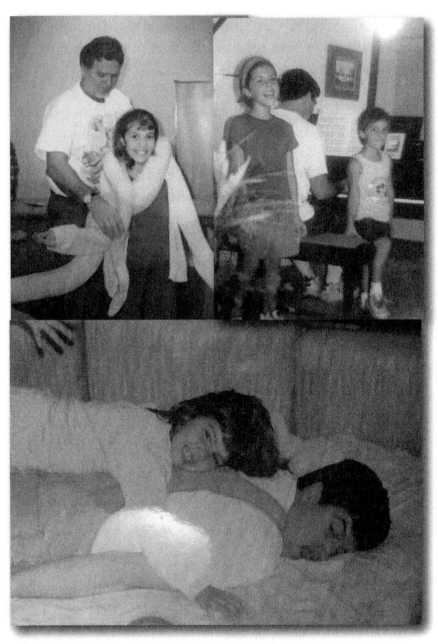

The PPEA also scheduled regular field trips to various places within Pinellas County. I remember one time we went to a farm and watched chicken eggs hatch. Another time we visited the water filtration plant and all the kids were grossed out by the smells of the water before it went through the filtration process. We also took some longer trips to explore the caves and quarries of Northern Florida. Those were always very exciting. I think we even kept some of the quarry stones in the garden by the pool. They may still be there, for all I know.

**Hands-in experience**

Children, below, learned how to make puppets duri Sunday at the Great Explorations Museum in St. P At left, Celeste Horsley helps daughter Michelle, 7

Once every month or so, we'd go to the Museum of Science and Industry (MOSI) or Great Explorations. We also took gymnastics at LaFleurs for a brief time, but I don't remember too much about it. It's at MOSI that Jason got really into chess. At one point during our childhood, there was a chess board - set up and ready to play - in every room of the house. We invested in one of the those transportable, all-in-one kits which had the cloth board and a bag for the pieces.

These were the standards which they used for official chess competitions.

Jason competed for many years against his own age group as well as many who were much older than he was (just for fun), and won tons of trophies. Dad used to joke that the trophies were bigger than he was. Dad competed too, but was never as successful as Jason was. Regardless, dad bought books and read up on trick plays and famous players throughout the ages. It's a fascinating game. Jason and dad shared some great memories playing it.

It was around this time that I also started getting very interested in birds. I'm still not really sure why or how. There were certainly plenty of them around our neighborhood, so I guess that must have helped. From the time I was very little, creating fantastical imaginary worlds in the front year with Aaron to Middle School when I got swept up into the Harry Potter craze, I suppose I was always fascinated by the concept of magical things. Birds were the most magical thing on Earth to me - the way they were so free and unique and musical. How could you not acknowledge the intrigue in that?

Throughout our entire childhood, really, Jason and I were constantly obsessed with something. There was a period in which we would go to construction sites on our street everyday to look for "fossils". For a while I was also infatuated with sea shells. I would leaf through National Geographic articles on all the different types of shells and how to find them. I had little sectionalized plastic boxes to organize the scallop shells from the conchs, the turkey wings from the whelks... Jason and I used to scoop out handfulls of sand in the sloppy, gushy part between the water and the dry beach to watch the dozens of colorful coquinas scramble to bury themselves back into the muck.

Anyway, the bird obsession was a long-lived phase. Christmas after Christmas, birthday after birthday, all I requested was bird-themed gifts. Grandma made me pillows with bird designs on them. I got stack upon stack of Audubon field guides. Mom and I re-landscaped the front yard with shrubbery like Crapemyrtles which were known to attract many birds. I would tediously plot out migratory paths and compile lists of birds for each season

or each climate. I must've memorized hundreds of different species; I even tried to learn some of their scientific names. It was a very serious and bizarre interest for a little kid.

We also joined other young homeschoolers in an ethnic dance group called SPICE (St. Petersburg International Children's Ensemble) under the direction of Mary Kruger. Each dancer had to wear a unique ethnic costume. After a year wearing a cheap Hawaiian dress, grandma Turner came to the rescue to sew a more appropriate European costume. I remember my frilly sleeves, the skirt that "finned" (past tense of "spin"), and the headband with the knit red flower.

# NEIGHBORHOOD IMAGES

**FOUR PARTNERS:** Ray Horsley of St. Petersburg dances with his children, Michelle, 6, and Jason, 3, on Saturday at the Third Annual Little Coliseum Ballroom. Michelle, dressed in Polynesian garb, performed at Oktoberfest with the St. Petersburg Children's Ensemble of the St. onal Folk Fair Society. The three-day Oktoberfest festival featured ethnic food, entertainment, yodeling and dancing.

We danced with that group year after year, getting progressively larger trophies at the end of each one. Eventually, Jason and I made it into the "older kids" group, which, of course, was a big deal. That was the group that Amanda Kruger - the dance instructor's daughter - was in. It also meant that we were suddenly adults, obviously. It was nothing in comparison to our own musical group within the family that performed at the same senior citizen venues, but it was still a creative outlet and it was fun. Dad used to get a kick out of how Mary Kruger would announce dance numbers the same way for each performance, in a storybook sort of style. "Now here we arrive in the beautiful land of Poland, where we see the beautiful countryside..."

Mom and dad also signed us up for swimming lessons at the YMCA where we progressed in our swimming skills with ranks, similar to those in boy scouts. When we passed the 200m dolphin stroke test, for example, we went from our guppy badge to our minnow badge. Ever since one particularly funny slip-of-the-tongue while we were getting on the highway, YMCA-bound, we always asked in unison, jokingly, "Are we swimming to going lessons?"

I don't remember exactly when in elementary school we started the gifted program at Sexton Elementary School, but it was very important because that is how we met the Adams Family. As the story goes, in 1997 on Amy's first

day day in the program, the teacher pointed at a girl on the other side of the classroom and told Amy to talk to her because she was nice. That girl was me. As Amy remembers it, we both said "hi" and then she asked, "Do you want to be friends?" Sometimes life really is that simple.

Our teacher, Mr. Pleshe, had us do all kinds of projects based on particular topics for each scholastic year. I remember one year we focused on the Native Americans. Amy and I dressed up as Sacajawea and built wigwams with toothpicks. Another year we studied Ancient Greece and I remember building a mini Coliseum out of clay and legos. One of my favorites was the year we studied dinosaurs and had to pick our favorite to present for the class at the end of the year. I chose Triceratops. Amy chose Brachiosaurus.

Amy and I were constantly hanging out. She would come over to our place and we'd have pizza parties. I'd go over to her house and we would explore in the field behind her house. She always dreamed of keeping a pony there. Many years later, Cracker Barrel decided to build a restaurant there and the field became a parking lot. The Adamses also had a pool. Amy and I used to sit around it during the summer and try to catch frogs.

We also shared a common interest in music and loved to do Disney sing-alongs. We could frequently be found dancing in their piano room, which was covered in mirrors, to the soundtrack of Pocahontas. As we became more proficient at our instruments, we would try playing some of our favorites tunes ourselves at the piano. Amy also became an excellent flautist and joined the Pinellas Youth Symphony years later.

During the 1990's, the television was becoming more and more of an invasive and addictive entertainment which plagued many homes. After just a few years, mom and dad decided instead to eliminate this from our house before it became a potential distraction from our time together as family. Dad worked it so that although we couldn't access any channels, we could still use the VCR to watch movies on VHS tapes. We would often rent movies from the video store on 62nd Avenue called Pot o' Gold Video, which was run by a guy named Dean who got to know our taste in movies very well over many years. I also remember the cost of renting a video was always a dollar and some menial amount of cents, like 4 cents. Whoever has 4 cents? Dad used to make us fish it out of the ashtray on our way to the video store; he hated having to deal with all the "chicken feed".

We'd also borrow educational tapes from the library. My favorite was always The Magic School Bus. Jason's was Bill Nye. A couple years later, we got really into old Laurel and Hardy episodes. Over the years, we must've seen every vignette they ever filmed. We kept stacks of their tapes which we would watch over and over while eating ice cream at the bar which separated the kitchen from the living room. Our favorites were the full movies (*Swiss Miss, Way out West, Babes in Toyland*, etc.) We were constantly quoting things from our favorites scenes. In fact, we still do.

Instead of TV, we resorted to more creative outlets. We played ridiculous games like Spider Hot Lava, in which the object was to travel throughout the house without touching the ground (which was obviously lava). Jason and I also built incredible "forts" out of cardboard boxes, blankets, string, and cushions. Sometimes we had more fun playing with the cardboard boxes in which gifts were wrapped than playing with gifts themselves. I remember that one Christmas, mom and dad gave us nothing but big pieces of cardboard and cushions taken from old couches. It was great! We created all sorts of crazy things. Mom was quick to break out the camcorder and interview us on our architectural accomplishments.

During our early childhood, dad was the Director of Music at Our Savior Lutheran Church & School, where he taught children music lessons. This was the first church where Jason and I really started performing. Jason used to sing the Mallot version of The Lord's Prayer during services, which would always bring people to tears. The pastor was always jealous that his sermons couldn't do the same. Dad put so many hours into his job at Our Savior Lutheran. He was constantly working on big programs and concerts. I remember one year we performed 100% Chance of Rain, a children's cantata which my grandfather wrote.

As with any class of children, there was always the troublemaker. One year, a kid by the name of Nicholas Obergon started getting on my dad's nerves because he was constantly doing things to seek attention. Sometimes, however, you just had to learn how to enjoy the child despite his obviously annoying tendencies. One day, while he was sitting in the corner of the room ("time-out" for something disruptive he had done), dad was teaching the rest of the class to sing the spiritual *Ezekiel Saw the Wheel*. Little Nicholas once again was getting himself into trouble by playing with a wheeled cart which happened to be within his reach. One of the wheels fell off which caused him to jump up and smile, exclaiming, "Look! The wheel!". Rachel Anderson was also another kid dad remembers fondly from his time at Our Savior. She came from a torn family and was constantly spending nights at her sister's house instead of home. One day, dad was casually talking to her about her sister, asking her what she did for a living. Rachel told him that she was a dancer. Dad was caught off guard by her following comment: "You should see the outfits she wears! You can see right through em!" Ah, the honesty of children.

# Chapter 3:
## The Band

One day, some people in the congregation invited us to sing for a local senior center for the folks there. Fred and Bunny performed regularly at a place called The Sunshine Center, which was right by Mirror Lake Library in downtown St. Petersburg. There was also a man named Rocky who played drums and was very encouraging of our early musical pursuits. His mother had Alzheimer's and lived in another center called Park Place where he asked us to perform. Those were our very first gigs.

At first it was just dad and me because Jason was too young. I was too young to really read, so dad wrote out sheets of early clipart pictures for me to learn the lyrics. For example, the first line of lyrics for "Tomorrow" (from the musical *Annie*) were "The sun will come out tomorrow; bet your bottom dollar that tomorrow, they'll be sun." That would be depicted by a picture of the sun, an arrow, a dollar bill, etc. Somewhere in the house, we still have a few of these.

Dad and I did this for a couple years until Jason was old enough to join. This duo would later include Jason to become The Horsley Trio, which was frequently taken into the streets as Two Bums and an Orphan and finally metamorphed into Two Bees and a Honey.

## Set List  November '02

Cabaret                                    B flat

*Intro
If I Were A Rich Man

It's a Sin To Tell A Lie

Let's Fall In Love

Foggy Day, Baby Face - Medicare

Anything Goes, One, Mame, Dolly

Let The Rest of the World Go By

El Rancho Grande

*Intro
Old Mother Hubbard

Singin' In The Rain/Good Morning

Born to Entertain

Lu Lu's Back in Town

*Intro
We're a Couple of Swells

## Set List  April '03

Cabaret                                    B flat

*Intro
If I Were A Rich Man                       B flat

It's a Sin To Tell A Lie                   B flat

Let's Fall In Love                         A flat

Foggy Day, Baby Face - Medicare            D flat, B flat

Bicycle Built for Two                      D maj

Anything Goes, One, Mame, Dolly            A flat, D flat, A flat, A flat

Let The Rest of the World Go By            E flat

El Rancho Grande                           E flat

*Intro
Old Mother Hubbard                         D

Singin' In The Rain/Good Morning           E flat/G maj

Born to Entertain                          B flat

Singin' In The Rain/Good Morning           E flat/G maj
I Love A Piano
Lu Lu's Back in Town                       C min

*Intro
We're a Couple of Swells                   R B♭

Now may be a good time to mention Ybor City, since it really jumpstarted this odd ability we developed as children to perform at the drop of a hat for strangers.

Since mom took off work to homeschool us during the week, she worked weekends instead, tempting dad to do all kinds of crazy adventures with us. I suppose that some of the things we did were fairly normal for kids our age. We took a couple trips to the zoo, museums, various parks and festivals. Other trips, however, were things that only the Horsleys would do.

Downtown St. Petersburg was a source of entertainment, but Ybor City was a *constant* source of entertainment. I'm not sure exactly when our escapades to Ybor started. Perhaps we weren't super little, but we were definitely young kids and it was never age-appropriate. Going to Ybor City would almost ensure that something crazy would happen. Ybor City wasn't a city at all; it was actually just one street - 7th Avenue - which was lined with nothing but filthy bars, raging discotheques, theaters, arcades, fancy restaurants, grungy restaurants, smoke shops, sex shops, hippie shops, protests, parades, you name it. Police would block off all the intersecting streets around 9pm so that 7th Avenue was totally car-free. All the drunks could dance and flail around freely.

There were certainly a number of staples in the scene - the "Jesus freaks," as we called them, who shouted Biblical condemnations from megaphones at the passing drunks; the flocks of tipsy female "flamingos" who poured their bodies into cling-wrap dresses and balanced precariously upon the skinniest and highest of heels; the dude groups of "duh"-faced men whose clothes were always too big and baggy and whose primitive demeanors we likened to those of Neanderthal, food-driven beings; the occasional but inevitable transvestite... Needless to say, it was always a colorful place to be.

In Ybor, we didn't even really need to *do* anything. Just being there guaranteed an eventful night. Sometimes when we'd see or hear something crazy, Jason would just shrug his shoulders dismissively and say, "Eh, it's Ybor City." Mom's shifts were always from 9am-11pm and it wouldn't be until nearly 1am that she would finish with charts and giving reports. It was always a race to see who would get home first - us or mom. Mom would always be disappointed with us if we were out later than she was and we would notoriously lose track of time while in Ybor. It ended up becoming somewhat of a challenge to see how much fun we could have before hurrying back home and quickly jumping under the covers to pretend we had been asleep for hours.

This continued for years and years. Sometimes the contagious, late-night atmosphere would make us compete with all the energy around us. Dad would just walk up to strangers, tap them on the shoulder and ask, "Hey guys, wanna hear a song?" and we'd all just burst into song. Other times we told jokes. Other times we danced. It really caught people off guard, but how could they say no? We became confident and wild; nothing phased us as being socially embarrassing. If it was fun, we did it. I'm not really sure what came first - the craziness with which we surrounded ourselves or the crazy family we became. Either way, as a young family, we were nuts and fearless. Even Ybor City couldn't handle us.

These impromptu "performances" became more and more of a regular idea, until one day dad decided to try it for money. Jason and I were really the stars of the act; all dad did was instigate and accompany. A keyboard wasn't the easiest instrument to transport, so one day dad noticed a huge, old, ridiculous-looking sousaphone in one of the closets at the church where he worked (now St. Paul United Methodist Church). Knowing that it wasn't worth much and would probably never be used there, he took the liberty of keeping it.

And so it was that one day we stood on the corner of 2nd Avenue NE and Beachshore Drive, with dad wielding a marching-band-like sousaphone while Jason and I sang old show tunes. Sure enough, people would stop to watch the spectacle and toss dollars at our feet. I remember that one of the first nights, we made over $60 in an hour (the equivalent of $100 today). This became not only a fun thing to do on the weekends, but also a prosperous business which afforded our nights out on the town. We called ourselves Two Bums and an Orphan. I was the orphan.

People really didn't know what to think when they came around the corner and saw a man and his two young children performing songs in the street. To this day, I haven't seen anything that even comes close to what we did. We just kept learning more and more songs.

In 1999, dad changed church jobs. He left Our Savior Lutheran Church and took a position at St. Paul United Methodist Church, which we fondly started referring to as "Glory Boy's". Unfortunately, the pastor was a very political, ego-driven man who required the rest of staff to be subservient. Our favorite quote from him, which perfectly describes his attitude was, "He's a good man; I've seem him cry."

There was certainly a lot in the church to go to his head. The congregation was huge and full of vibrant families. There was a large, dedicated choir. Several Sunday services were broadcast on television. Pastor Tom would plan specific moments of his weekly sermons in which he would cry. He would cry at the same time for both the early and late services. Dad thought this kind of "performance" was just disgusting and was appalled that nobody else in the church seemed to realize the ridiculousness of it all. But, it was a job and the money was good. He kept his frustrations to himself and once we got home on Sunday afternoons, we'd all laugh about it over lunch and a bottle of wine.

Dad continued working there until sometime in 2000 when he just couldn't handle the pastor any longer. I remember having to sit through a grueling midnight service on New Year's Eve (who holds a church service on New Year's Eve?!) and sleepily watching the scattered bunches of fireworks light up the skyline as we drove home that night. Despite the conviction in his sermons, the pastor was terrified that there would be a terrorist attack on the eve of the millennium. He didn't let dad play "He's Got the Whole World in His Hands", because he was afraid that the song lyrics would be proved wrong.

If nothing else, we did get the sousaphone from that church, which resulted in some very entertaining evenings. One time when grandma and grandpa Turner were visiting, we took them and the sousaphone to what used to be The Oyster Bar in Ybor City. It was a grand night of storytelling and partying, ultimately leading to our family providing entertainment for the entire restaurant. Dad played oom-pa-pa accompaniments while Jason and I confidently walked right up to every table, addressing strangers individually through song. People didn't know what to think; everyone laughed and had a grand old time.

These years would become the height of Two Bees and a Honey. For many years, we had multiple gigs every weekend, with a particularly busy schedule during the winter holidays. In the weeks leading up to Christmas, we sometimes had shows everyday! We produced promotional videotapes of our act and handed out business cards whenever we could. We even bought wireless headsets and our own sound gear so we weren't ever dependent on whatever equipment the venue had or didn't have.

Once, we even hired a choreographer to give us a couple tips. Because of the nature of our repertoire - constantly changing between styles, solos to duets, comedic numbers to ballads - she suggested we have some sort of prop by which we could also aesthetically mirror our musical diversity. She recommended we place a hat rack on the side of the stage. For each song, we would change hats to fit the material. We thought it was a great idea.

We had around a dozen goofy hats, each paired with appropriate songs. Loading up the car for shows became second nature. We dismantled the hat rack, tossed all the hats in an old black duffle bag, (which I think mom and dad used many years prior for their scuba diving adventures), carefully placed the headsets in their little padded boxes, delicately tucked in the mic monitors, and any additional speakers or cables. Dad sometimes took a couple fake books, just in case. Other than that, we just had one piece of paper - a set list - which we catered to each gig. Jason and I usually stuck to it, but things often changed and in show biz, one must always be flexible. I'll always remember dad eagerly shouting out, "It's show time!" at the beginning of each gig.

Some of our favorite venues were The Vineyard Inn and Top of the World, but we still performed at The Sunshine Center and Park Place. Residents of these centers got to know us over the years. We'd get asked to perform for all kinds of crazy events. Sometimes for Christmas, we would have to sing on top of a moving truck during a parade. Another time, we performed for a huge convention of teachers. People would recognize us in the streets when we went out. Sometimes it felt like we had become local celebrities.

Of course we had disaster performances. We were constantly falling off stages, tripping during dance numbers, or forgetting words to songs. Jason was particularly adventurous when he forgot lyrics. He'd often try to make up his own on the spot. No shame at all. People loved it. Other times, he'd start scat-singing à la Ella Fitzgerald. "Sca-doodly doo bop da scooby doo bop!" He would walk right up to people and sit in their laps during songs. If ever we had a spotlight, there was no way of keeping up with him.

One particularly funny gig was in Seminole in which Jason was not in the best of health. He got nauseous on the drive over, so we stopped in the closest parking lot, which happened to be for a Chinese buffet restaurant. Sure enough, as soon we opened the car doors, Jason spewed all over the ground. Poor guy. Coincidentally, the sides of the restaurant were covered in huge windows, so everybody dining that particular afternoon got to enjoy Jason's lovely outdoor performance. As much as we tried to prevent it, Jason's clothes ended up getting very messy and we simply could not perform in them. The only place nearby happened to be CVS, a convenience store, in which the only clothes they had were cheap pajamas in army fatigue colors. We laughed at the ridiculousness of it and bought them.

By the time we arrived, Jason was feeling much better, with the exception of his wardrobe situation. He frantically ran his messy dress pants under the faucet in the bathroom, but there was no method or time to dry them. We scrambled to set up equipment and started wondering why Jason was taking so long in the bathroom. We found him later in a small exercise room which he had discovered down the hall. In a poor demonstration of scientific knowledge, he was smashing his dress pants with a weight machine, in efforts to squeeze the water out. Although it was obviously not working as he had hoped, it was a very entertaining effort. The show had to go on. Our performance was interrupted only by our fits of giggles at the situation itself. We tried explaining the story on stage as to why Jason was dressed so poorly. Everyone laughed it off and we had a great time.

One day at Largo Park when we were there socializing with other homeschoolers, Jason had a little bit of a disagreement with a tree. There were little tracks which were woven through the park on which people were driving miniature trains. Jason and his friends were chasing each other through the trees and got distracted by the trains. Jason also had the tendency to bob his head when he ran. I haven't seen him run in a long time and I wonder if he still does. Anyway, lesson learned; never run in one direction while facing another. Jason hit a tree straight on and started bleeding profusely from his forehead. I remember spotting him through the branches and screaming in horror. We scrambled to dry the wound with paper towels and immediately left for medical attention.

As everyone knows, a head wound is very serious and bleeds a lot. We had no idea of the level of severity, so we expected the worst and tried our hardest to keep Jason mentally awake while we waited for stitches. We sang through lyrics and asked him dumb questions about who he was, where he was, what had happened, etc. He was actually quite fine and just looked at us like we were idiots for asking him such stupid things. A few stitches later, he was fine, despite the horrendous scar. To this day, if you look really carefully, you'll still notice a little white scar around Jason's left eyebrow.

Naturally, our audiences were very curious and concerned about Jason's face. We capitalized on the situation and created a very detailed story of how Jason had gotten into a terrible fight with an alligator. From what I can remember, we were tossing around a football in the park near our home and it landed in by the lake. An alligator got a hold of it and Jason tugged and pulled and eventually got the football loose. "If you think I look bad, you should've seen that alligator!" he exclaimed. Always true to his art; what a showman.

# Chapter 4:
## Interests and Adventures

Jason was always very interested in video games. During the 1990s, we used to play Oregon Trail. Later he got into games like Bugdom, Cro-Mag Rally, and Roller Coaster Tycoon. Later still, he played games like Jak and Daxter.

Throughout middle school, Jason and I both got into a game called Dance Dance Revolution, which involved physically stepping on a mat to corresponding arrows on the screen. Mom and dad's main concern with video games was that they were stationary forms of entertainment, so naturally they loved the concept of DDR. It was very popular in early 2000s and we were very, very good at it. For several Christmases we got newer versions of the game. We had several dance pads at home and were constantly inviting the Adamses, the Simpsons, or the McCormicks to play with us. We used to go to arcades like Gameworks in Ybor City to show off dancing to Max 300 on expert level. Oh man, good times.

As kids, we were so involved with extra-curricular activities that it's almost easier to discuss what we *didn't* do. For a couple years, we took tennis lessons with Jennifer Dietrich downtown in Northshore Park. Jason and I also took art lessons from this crazy lady named Boo at a building in Pinellas Park which they later tore down to make a giant, stupid clock. We worked with paints, colored pencils, and Sculpey clay. Usually I would just draw pictures of birds or Dolly, our dog. We did one cool project of creating our own board games. We even sculpted the dice and playing pieces. I remember one of Boo's own paintings - a purple bath tub in a forest. I don't know why that sticks in my memory, but it does.

A couple consecutive summers were spent at Boyd Hill Nature Park learning how to do all kinds of pioneer-themed things like churning butter and baling hay. We regularly attended the Florida State Fair, where our favorite exhibit was always Cracker Country. One year, this inspired dad to start wearing overalls for whatever reason. He must've worn these ratty jean overalls everyday for months. It was not particularly flattering or stylish.

I have no idea how or why it started, but one day Jason became obsessed with digging holes in our front yard. It started as a little project in which mom wanted him to replant some bushes. One thing led to another and he ended up getting really carried away with the shovel. We were always very curious kids and I suppose that may have been what drove us to do such things. As the hole got deeper and deeper, it became a little hiding spot for us to hang out. Cars passing by couldn't see us. With all the time we were spending out there, dad started getting concerned that one day the hole might cave in on us. He started setting limits as to how deep we could dig, but I don't think we heeded his authority very well. One day we went outside to find that they had filled it in with dirt while we were sleeping. This, of course, was devastating. Thankfully, we never got hurt by wielding shovels nor did we ever suffocate under collapsed piles of dirt.

Dad had a better idea for front-yard activities. He tied some sturdy ropes between two of the largest trees in our yard and then suspended a gigantic tire which traveled along a pulley from one tree to the other. We spent countless hours on our homemade tire-swing. The tire ended up getting punctured and deflated, but we continued playing on it like nothing had happened. Eventually it became just a swingable rubber stub. After many years of swinging around like monkeys, the whole set-up had to be taken down. The city of St. Petersburg was constantly forcing us to carve around one of the trees because it was too close to the power lines along the street. After we were forced into a particularly horrible tree-trimming job which left the poor oak looking mutilated, we decided it was time for it to be cut down. Mom cried the day it was removed. It was a beautiful tree and there were so many great memories. The other tree was closer to the house and left untouched. If you look closely, you can still see where the tree grew around the rope.

Just as Jason and I would go through phases of interests in bizarre activities or things, dad also developed some rather unique hobbies. For a while, he became completely obsessed with spicy food. We would take a trip to the pier just to buy his favorite Lotti's hot sauce (or his second favorite, called "Screaming Sphincter"). When purchasing hot sauce no longer did it for him, he turned to planting his own hot peppers. He and mom planted progressively spicier plants from jalapeños to tabascos to the ultimate and spiciest of them all - the habañero.

Sailing became a pretty serious hobby over the years. We took lessons downtown at the Sailing Center, where they started us out on boats called Optis, which were one-man, introductory sailboats. We eventually graduated to 420s - named after their dimensions (4.2 meters in length). They were slightly larger, 2-person dinghies. I think at one point we actually bought our own Opti. Dad always shared in our interests and decided to learn how to sail with us. He ultimately bought a 14' Puffer sailboat which, for many years, was our go-to weekend activity. We'd pack a lunch and take her out into Tampa Bay or the

Gulf of Mexico for a few hours. It was no easy cruise, mind you; sailing involved very tedious effort. Many times we capsized, but it was only scary the first couple times. By standing on the overturned dagger board, we used our body weight to right the boat.

During our little sailing adventures, we would often find ourselves on islands completely inhabited by birds and mangroves. We joked about conquering these bits of land and calling them our own. I think we even decided to claim one of them and name it Jamray Island (a combination of letters in our names). It was never unusual to see dolphins and stingrays in the waters surrounding Tampa Bay. A few times we even spotted sharks. Once when dad took it out by himself, he got within arms-reach of a sea turtle. It was an incredible experience for him.

It should come as no surprise that Jason and I were involved in theatre productions around the area. For a couple years, Jason and I were involved in a community theatre which cast people of all ages. Jason scored the part of Scrooge for their Christmas Story production. His energetic performance brought the house down. During one of  the performances, in a scene in which he had to put on a night cap, his old-man wig fell off his head. Instead of trying to dismiss the mishap, Jason capitalized on its comedic value - his reaction was priceless and everyone watching burst into fits of laughter.

Jason and I also performed with a group called Bravo, a musical theatre program for kids. That year we did the musical *Annie*, and I was cast as the mean orphanage lady (Miss Hannigan) and Jason was cast as Rooster (ironically, also siblings). Our good friends, Megan and Kelly Simpson, also attended the program. They had danced with us previously during our years with SPICE as well. We also somehow got involved in a production of *Lil' Abner* in which we had to dress like country bumpkins and talk with a hick accent.

As homeschoolers, our curriculum was chosen by mom. It was sometimes difficult for her to relate with the other homeschoolers because it was such an eccentric bunch. Many people homeschooled because they were religious fanatics who thought even Christian schools were not Christian enough. There was plenty of diverse curriculum to chose from. Mom ended up liking the Calvert books and we stuck with them for many years. In middle school, mom imported math books for us from Singapore, where their math level was superior to that of the USA. Although some of the word problems in the pre-algebra books had comical English translations, the content was really quite good and we learned a lot.

Every year we would get tested by a man named Dennis Apple. He gave us all kinds of out-of-the-box tests which supposedly indicated the grade level at which we were performing for each core subject. Jason and I constantly scored into grade levels much higher than our own.

A strange memory which sticks with me this day was one day when Paul Lewis, a fellow homeschooler, came over to play. I don't remember ever getting that close to him as a friend, but apparently as very little kids we got together often. Anyway, he and I were in the hallway and he suddenly got all awkward and weird. He asked me if I wanted to do the "K word". I had no idea what he was talking about. Frustrated, he started spelling, "k-i-s...". "No!", I yelled. I'm so glad that didn't actually become my first kiss.

After our dogTina died, mom and dad made a visit to our local animal shelter and found another dog. They picked a little energetic mutt and let me choose her name. I named her after my favorite musical during the time, *Hello Dolly*. She was such a great dog and we made lovely memories with her. Dolly accompanied us on some of our wild weekend adventures to Ybor City and she even made it into some of our art. There's a colored pencil drawing of her which hangs in our kitchen today.

I remember one time when Dolly was still a puppy. She was chasing her tail and actually caught it. The silly creature bit down so hard that one of her baby teeth fell out. I thought it was so hilarious.

The most dramatic story about Dolly was the time when we were hosting another Terry/Adams/Horsley party. There were so many people around the house and somebody must have forgotten to latch the little hinged gate in the front yard. Dolly sneaked out and started exploring the neighborhood. Shortly after, we all started wondering where she was. While a couple of us left in search of her, a couple police officers knocked on our door. "Do you guys have a little brown dog?" "Yes, officer. Why?" "Well, she got squished."

Despite the horrific news (and the horrific delivery of it), Dolly ended up being okay. Her broken hind leg needed to be in a cast for a while, but she recovered without any complications, smiling all the way.

Mom and dad took us
on tons of camping trips throughout Florida. We
frequented the KOA campgrounds, which were rated as
both family and dog friendly. At all costs, we avoided those
stupid RV camps. Who wants to go into nature just to sit
inside of a vehicle, anyway? Fort de Soto was a nearby
campground which we visited often. It was completely
infested with very extroverted raccoons, which made for
some entertaining animal vs. human interaction.

One time, after doing all the work to set up the tents and pin them into the ground, the wind picked up dramatically and we decided we would rather be on the other side of the campground, away from the windy shore. Not wanting to throw away all our work of tediously assembling our campsite, we simply decided to lift the tent on the roof of our car and drive it to the other side. It was quite the ridiculous site, and all the other campers who happened to be watching were stunned by our efforts.

For most of our childhood, we had two cars. One was a white 1988 Crown Victoria, which is the stereotypical old cop car, found in movies like The Blues Brothers. The other car was a blue Caprice Classic from around the same year. It had a unique look, complete with the cool silver part that overlapped the top of the two back wheels. We must have put so many miles on those cars. Eventually, the cloth ceiling in the Caprice started losing its stickiness and gradually fell down. We had to have a stash of tacks to keep it pinned up. There were many jokes made about the likelihood of sitting on a fallen tack.

Gosh, we went on so many adventures. One year, dad decided to take the whole family on a cruise, which is something none of us had ever done and considered to be quite a luxury. Many months in advance, dad booked us a trip on Carnival's Tropicale, which was a week-long voyage to the Virgin Islands and back. The night before we were to set sail, however, we received a 5am phone call alerting us that the ship had experienced a fire in the kitchen and was no longer fit to sail. We went to the port where we would have left and the company gave us a refund to use on a different cruise. We ended up the Big Red Boat, a Looney Tunes themed ship with life-sized cartoons running all over the boat at any given time. It was quite a trip. We never made it to the Virgin Islands, but our spontaneous trip to the Bahamas ended up being a ton of fun. Jason was quick to tell the other passengers that we would have taken a different cruise, but it "burnt down".

Despite being homeschooled, Jason and I had some very good, close friends. Through the same program in which Amy and I met, Jason became good friends with Joey Garrison (who now goes just by "Joe"). Joey was also homeschooled and they spent many afternoons together, playing games or sports.

Another favorite pastime was to attend the annual Bay-area Renaissance Festival. We went year after year, with either the Terrys, the McCormicks, or the Adamses. It was always fun to meet the king and queen, who always had words of wisdom to impart. One of dad's favorite quotes was when the king made a rather profound remark upon being asked what about his favorite restaurant. "Good, fast and cheap. One can never have all three. If you have good and fast, the food is not cheap. If you have cheap and fast, the food is not good. " For many years, we tried to prove him wrong, but I'm not sure we ever did. After all, he was a very wise king.

If we were lucky, we would spend Christmases in Chicago, visiting mom's family and dad's old friends. We were always tempted to avoid the cost of a hotel and stay with grandma and grandpa in their huge house on Hoyne, but the cat shed everywhere and it was an awful combination for the allergies that both dad and I sometimes suffered from. Ultimately we found a conveniently located Day's Inn and, although management shifted several times over the years, the staff remained and remembered us, year after year. How could they not remember us? We always sang to them.

It was always great to visit the Turner clan. Grandpa was always the quiet, thoughtful one, with an undeniable silly streak which could light a whole room with smiles. He was always tinkering with some odd contraption, creating another bizarre vehicle out of used bicycles and car batteries. (The most memorable of these was, of course, the famous Quadricycle.) It caused such a spectacle when we drove the things to the park. At any given time, you could find over a hundred broken bicycles in his back yard. He fixed bikes and donated them to needy kids - a hobby that gained him recognition not only in the neighborhood, but also the newspaper, heralding him as the "bike man".

Grandma has always had a heart of gold and was always telling wild, unbelievable stories. She was an extremely compassionate woman who never hesitated to take people in if they needed help. There was constantly coffee on the stovetop and pies on the counter. Without a doubt, that house always was and still is such a loving place.

The family was large and diverse. There were always interesting developments about new jobs, babies, marriages, etc. There was always more than plenty to talk about.

Among dad's friends, there were also plenty of characters. Through the year, we've enjoyed the company of the Beshoars and the Eckwalls. We also always made an effort to visit Jim Cannon ("Jimmer") who was an eclectic musician, old friend, and probably the only man in the world who could compete with dad in goofiness.

It seemed like we all shared in the child-like humor, even mom. In a way, dad was no more mature than we were. We embraced the goofiness, the craziness, the contagious, uncontainable energy about life together.

# Chapter 5:
## Around the Millennium

And so it was through the turn of the millennium. Two Bees and a Honey was very active, with shows every weekend and an ever-expanding repertoire. Homeschooling was at its height, with mom devoting every day to our education and weekends to her job. Dad was completely self-employed and now making a living by selling LinkIt, a software program which he created. We were very close with the Adamses, the Terrys, the McCormicks, the Simpsons, the Garrisons, and the Jocelyns. We were a busy family.

As I entered 6th grade, mom and dad encouraged me to get involved with Meadowlawn Middle School, which was my zoned school. We found an all-girls choir called The Lancerettes and so I joined. Previously, I had sung with Rick Smith's adult choir at First Presbyterian Church downtown St. Petersburg. I was probably the only singer under 30 years old, but I had no problem establishing camaraderie. The alto section was very welcoming and filled with wonderful people. We did great anthems and it was a joy to sing under such a talented and fun conductor. I decided to try another chorus, this time with people my own age.

The Lancerettes were directed by a lady named Andrea Clemmens and, although very strict, she was loved by the kids she conducted. Once a year, both the choir itself and individual members thereof were encouraged to participate in Thespians, which were competitions for performing arts. Dad convinced me to try my own solo act for the Thespians, so I learned a song called "I was Born to Entertain." We choreographed it and dad accompanied. There were four possible ratings: poor, fair, excellent, and superior. I was thrilled to get all excellents for the regional division and then superiors for the state division! My peers supported me and we all had a great time throughout the scholastic year.

Around this time, Jason and I had transitioned from piano lessons to organ lessons. (Our legs were finally long enough to reach the pedals.) We were quickly becoming quite proficient and by 2000, we were able to help dad by playing the entirety of the Lent services at Bethel Lutheran Church, where he worked. I still remember the first hymns I learned - the ones we had to play every week for the Lenten services. (*O Sacred Head Now Wounded*, *How Firm a Foundation*, and *Rock of Ages*)

The story of how dad got the job at Bethel Lutheran in 2000 is a kind of funny one. One night as we were walking through the parking lot of Dean's Pot o' Gold Video, dad saw the church on the other side of the street and decided to inquire about it. He walked across the street, had one simple conversation with a man named Art Bleasey, and got the job.

Anyway, it was in that church, on that little 2-manual Rodgers instrument, that Jason and I really started learning how to play the organ. The church was so close to our house that sometimes we would just walk over. We practiced, as usual, every night for an hour each. Dad would sometimes get a little bored and sneak a sip of communion wine from the sacristy.

Both Jason and I were close with the Terry family during this time - another friendship that would last a lifetime. Josh, their youngest, was my age (and still is), but played equally well with both Jason and me. Josh's two older brothers, Eli and John, also frequented our house when we would throw holiday parties. Mom and dad became good friends with their parents, Kathy and Joe, who were also homeschoolers. Together, we attended various PPEA functions and trips.

Mom had started using math books from Singapore to teach me Algebra. Their level of math education was higher than that of the USA, so although the English translations for word problems were comically bad, the content itself was very good. I remember that they were orange books and had lots of little people figures in them, all of which looked distinctly Asian.

Although we were no longer in Elementary School and therefore didn't have Gifted class together, Amy Adams and I were still great friends and got together regularly. She attended St. Petersburg Christian School, which was also in the immediate neighborhood. We would go ice-skating at the old Pinellas Park Mall (now Park Side, a dumb outdoor strip mall).

Amy and I still had sleepovers and still sang along to Disney movies. Now we were able to accompany each other on the piano to some of our favorite musicals,

*Chicago* and *The Sound of Music.* I used to love waking up to the sound of Amy's dad playing the piano.

It was also around this time that I discovered I needed glasses. Mom, always the observant caretaker, was surprised when I couldn't read a road sign one day while we were driving down I275. She made me get my eyes examined and, sure enough, -1.00 and -1.25 in left and right eyes, respectively.

Dad, Jason, and I still had our adventures on the weekends while mom worked. For a while, we had season tickets to the Florida Orchestra and would attend a concert every weekend. Sometimes, if the concerts were particularly amazing, once a week was just not enough. We'd attend the Friday night performance and then decided to come back for the Saturday and Sunday performances as well.

Naturally, our tickets only allotted one showing of each, so we would just casually stand around in front of the concert hall and wait for people to give up tickets. We had various strategies and sometimes waited until minutes before the concert started, sure that there was no way we could possibly end up getting in again for free. But, miraculously, it worked out every time. We ended up falling in love with so many great pieces. We particularly loved the piano concerti by Rachmaninov. Dad would buy CDs of each and play them around the house for weeks prior to the concerts. (We greatly preferred these over that stupid Wyndom Hill elevator music.) By the time we heard the music live, we had to almost keep ourselves from singing along.

Our favorite restaurants during this time were still Luby's (on 9th Street) and Picadilly's, where all four of us would eat several courses for about $18 total. I still remember the silliest things - those big round designs on the carpet, the Asian server with the huge fake breasts, etc.

Around this time, we also signed up for memberships at the YMCA, where we took swimming lessons many years prior (in its old downtown location). For our membership cards, each of us followed dad's example of making the most ridiculous face when they took our pictures. Every time we entered the building, we had to line up and swipe our cards on the desk in front of the secretary. Our pictures would appear on a huge computer screen for everyone to see. What a family of goofs.

In the summer of 2000, we decided to take a little trip to beautiful Savannah, Georgia. Like many kids my age during this time, I was completely obsessed with the Harry Potter series. I remember that I started and finished the 5th Harry Potter book (*Order of the Phoenix*) during the train ride there. I read it again, cover to cover, on the train ride back.

By the river in Savannah, the streets are lined with quaint candy shops and old cafes. There's a long winding park parallel to the river which is always filled with street musicians and caricature artists.

You can feel the city's soul under its uneven, leaf-littered bricks.

On our first night there, we had dinner at a little restaurant by the water. Dad always loved long, unhurried meals. (I think that's the main reason why any celebratory dinner in our family usually involved snow crab; it takes forever to eat!) Anyway, this was that kind of a meal. It involved many courses and much conversation. We gabbed on for over an hour, probably laughing about ridiculous pastors we had worked for or funny stories from our various gigs. Dad probably sang his orders to the waiter, which was very typical for him to do.

When we finally asked for the bill, the waiter casually informed us that it had already been paid. An elderly woman who had eaten alone a few tables away had paid the entirety of our meal. She had commented to the waiter that she had never seen a family have so much fun together and was very touched by it. We immediately ran down the street, trying to find this mystery woman, but to no avail. She didn't want to be thanked. We had never experienced that kind of anonymous gift and it left quite an impression on all of us.

The weekend adventures to Ybor City never really stopped. Once, we decided it would be fun to try to sneak Dolly, our dog, into bars. We had three ways of doing this. One way was to simply approach the bouncer, point up and say, "Hey, look at that!", while dashing inside with the dog. That obviously didn't work. The other idea was to put Dolly in an empty printer box and just tell the bouncer that we were delivering their printer. This also proved unsuccessful. The method which did work - miraculously -

was actually to cover the dog in a blanket and play it off that she was our baby. This worked three times, but I still don't know how.

Sometimes we'd walk down the canal to the St. Pete Ale House on weeknights. We'd always ask for them to show our ale house favorite which was *The Agony of Defeat* - essentially a video compilation of hilarious sports bloopers. We kept looking for it in video stores, but could never find it outside of the ale house. Since we didn't have TV, we spent several solemn hours watching news footage at the Ale House on 9/11.

We continued our outings to downtown, constantly dancing in the streets, telling jokes to strangers, always stopping for late-night pizza at Fortunato's (which still, amazingly, exists!). Dad continued to be involved in occasional performances at First Presbyterian, where we were very good friends with their longtime organist, Jack Rein. Jason and I even performed on the organ for their annual Halloween concerts. One year, I performed a comical organ medley called *Nautical Extravaganza*. Even Jack Rain got dressed for the occasion and the whole congregation loved it.

Mom and dad starting doing remodeling of the pool area during these years. The wooden slats were old and had splinters. It was sad, in a way, to have to take those old slats out. The lizards loved crawling around under them and as kids we used stand very still and wait for the lizards to climb up our outstretched hands. Black ants didn't bite, so sometimes we would lure them by putting ants in our palms. We named our favorites Lizzie, Larry and The V (his tail was shaped like a V).

Anyway, it all had to ultimately go so we could replace it with a concrete deck. We each drew our names and placed our right hands into the wet concrete on the shower side. The last time I visited home, I put my hand down on the handprints. It's now twice the size of its old childhood imprint.

I think it was around this time that I finally learned that the word was "wallet," not "walnut". Dad always referred to it as his "walnut" and it led to a couple embarrassing misunderstandings later on.

In the summer of 2001, we took a little trip to Miami. Jason and dad took the train down first; mom and I drove down later. We were inspired by the multicultural environment and although we ended up late at night in some questionable areas of the city, it was overall a fun trip.

In 2002, dad took a position at Peace Memorial Presbyterian Church in Clearwater. It was directly across the street from the world headquarters for scientology. The pastor used to pull this infantile stunt of ringing the church bells really loudly when he knew their services were about to start - just to piss them off a little bit. Jason and I spent many hours practicing the organ there and we got very used to the long drive down US-19. We always went through the back door of the little cafe by the church parking lot to get bourbon chicken. Sometimes we'd walk down to Starbucks and get those caramel squares that are impossible to eat.

Dad's choir at Peace Memorial had lots of characters and one of our favorites was Claire Bernius. She was an old sweetheart with a wobbly voice who was constantly going out of her way to help out around the church. One time, we saw her carrying a huge vat of soup that she had made so she could help feed the homeless in Fellowship Hall.

Anyway, we discovered that she had been told by the previous director of music to stand but not to sing - something we found to be rude and outrageous. After much coercion, dad got Claire to sing a solo on Christmas Eve of 2003, which was a very special moment for not only her but the church. She died exactly ten years later.

Another character of the church was a man named Johnny who had the token title of "music librarian" and constantly was in need of something to do. Dad recognized this and one day gave him the small task of making copies of an anthem he had written (*I Heard the Voice of Jesus Say*). From downstairs, we suddenly heard a thump and the poor guy had fallen and dropped all the copies in a huge pile on the floor. Dad felt awful about the fall and so that weekend we bought him a cart to carry all the music, engraved with his name on the side. It was an unexpected and touching moment for him when the whole choir presented him with it.

As with any church, it had a handful of people who were difficult to work with. Ray Quiles, who had recently been promoted and was tempted to usurp even more control. Around the house, we referred to him as Ray Brainless. One time, Quiles went above dad's head to pay organ tuners who had actually done nothing but damage the instrument, leaving dad with not only an out-of-tune organ, but also no more money in the budget to fix it. Needless to say, he was a frustrating individual to work beside.

But, after all, it was church work and working for a church meant working with people. The church allotted for many very positive experiences as well. Jason and I spent countless hours practicing on that organ and singing in dad's choir. As always, we didn't really realize it at the time, but dad was teaching us invaluable skills and we were growing together even more.

# Chapter 6:
# Changes

2003 was the year that grandpa Horsley died. It was a very strange and surreal time. We had enjoyed so many trips to Cape Coral to visit the two of them on holidays. He had served as the director of music for churches throughout his whole life and he loved the fact that we were always so involved with music. He came to almost every church dad worked for during our childhood and could sit for hours just listening to us play the organ.

When we visited them, dad always made me sing "Somewhere Over the Rainbow" before we left. As I got older, I became sometimes reluctant to sing for him. I didn't understand how important it was and how much it meant to him. Now I wish I had sung more.

It wasn't until grandpa was gone that we realized how much he had held the extended family together. In his presence, he made it difficult for anybody to be in a sour mood. From his beautiful garden which wrapped around the house to cracking fresh macadamia nuts on the vice-grip in his shed to splashing around on pool noodles, everything was done with smiles and grandma's famous monkey bread.

I remember going into that little closet in their guest bedroom and fishing out tapes of Disney's *Fantasia* and dancing to them in the living room. I remember playing with all those decorative trinkets that grandma placed around the house. I remember looking through all her old jewelry while she told me stories about each piece. We always held hands and said grace before meals. It was this little sing-song which I can almost remember. Something like, "we thank you, Lord, for daily bread, for loving grace and .... we thank you, heavenly father, amen."

Grandma was always in the kitchen preparing something. In the evenings, we'd stroll past the neighborhood's burrowing owls to Starcastle Playground. Sometimes we'd visit the local pet shop and listen to the Kookaburra. Mostly though, grandpa would sit on the pool deck, chuckling about some old jokes and telling me I was a mermaid. He'd sit on the rocking lanai furniture and reminisce for hours with my dad while the obnoxious pet conure - Connie - shrieked in the background.

The last time we saw him was when he drove up for dad's 50th birthday. He climbed out of their Grand Marquis carrying huge balloons in one hand and balancing a cake in the other. A couple months later he fell asleep and didn't wake up. The very last thing he did was attend a Thursday evening choir practice - something we consider so symbolic of his life as a musician, especially since it was a rehearsal, not a performance. He had a very large life, filled with songs and people. I'm upset that he never got to know about our move to Spain, my pursuit of music as a career, etc. As always, we all just wanted more time.

I was too young still to really understand what happened then. When grandma called that early morning, voice shaking, telling us that grandpa wouldn't wake up and that she was so very sorry for inconveniencing us by calling, dad put down the phone and told us to pack a change of clothes and get in the car. We drove down and sat in the hospital for hours. He was gone, although still breathing with the help of a machine. His soul had already left and his body was weirdly warm and puffy. After a couple painful, confusing days, we ultimately had to make the decision that many families have to make. We let him go.

Love ya, Grandpa.

The story of what really happened after grandpa's death is one that is best explained late at night over a couple beers. For years we have all tried to understand exactly how everything happened and how dad's extended family fell apart. Ultimately I think it all can be traced back to the fragility of our human relationships and our obsessive desire for control. After lots of late-night pool deck conversations, rationalizing and remembering and trying to put pieces together, time inevitably passed and dust settled - at least for the time being.

In the summer of 2002, we visited Ghost Ranch by Albuquerque, New Mexico. We had originally planned on

just staying for two weeks, but ended up extending it to a month. Mom took stained glass classes and dad was able to do work from the campground on his computer, taking frequent breaks to hike up deadly mountains without any water. There were plenty of activities and programs for kids. I was even able to organize an ornithology group of adults which I led on birdwatching day-trips.

The camp was full of characters of all ages and everyone would get freaked out by the occasional bear alert. Mount Pedernal loomed ever-present in the distance and there were always picturesque treks up Chimney Rock.

When we returned, Bethel Lutheran had merged with another church and changed its name to Hope Lutheran Church. We enjoyed reuniting with the wonderful families there - the Herzhausers, the Bartelts, among many others.

Dad's software, LinkIt, which he had built from scratch and had made a living by selling to various school districts in the south, had gotten noticed by more than just the schools to which he sold it. A publishing company in New York City called Metro Publishing took an interest in it around this time and offered to buy it from him. While Jason and I would be practicing the little 2-manual Rodgers organ at Hope Lutheran, dad would be in the church's parking lot, on the phone in tedious negotiations. The negotiations lasted for about a year.

Luckily, dad had good friends he could call to ask for advice regarding big business negotiations of this type. With their help he was able to see how Metro essentially tried to initially steal the company out from under him in the preliminary negotiations. Dad stayed on his toes after that. About a year later, they signed a deal. Ever since then, dad has worked for Josh, who has represented the publishing company. He knows LinkIt better than anyone in the company; he has worked with them to improve and adapt it to ever-changing demands in the educational technology field.

In the summer of 2003, Jason and I attended Friends Music Camp. It was a month-long Quaker music camp in the middle of rural Ohio. The kids and teachers were all very kind and talented; it was a beautiful place to be. I took voice and piano lessons - there was no organ on which to take lessons - and Jason took piano lessons. We all performed in that year's musical, *Children of Eden*.

We began and ended every day by sitting with the entire camp in silence for 20 minutes - part of the Quaker religion. If anyone had something they felt like sharing during this time, they were welcome to. Sometimes people would stand up and say something lovely about how much they were touched by the music that day or the friendships they had formed. Although we were all uneasy about this tradition at first, I think everyone grew to accept it and even enjoy it. I particularly liked it.

I don't remember what piano pieces I worked on during the month, but I do remember in my voice lessons that I performed the song *From a Distance*. It was right around a C5, where my voice broke from chest to falsetto. We tried and tried to disguise it. (I still can't disguise it.)

Then we got the infamous letters. Mom and dad sent Jason and me one letter each, casually informing us that we would be moving. The name of the location where we would be moving was encrypted in a code of numbers and letters which we had to decipher by combining both of our letters. I actually stole Jason's letter from his mailbox, cracked the code and phoned home immediately. "Where in the world is Segovia???" It may have been that same day that I performed, *From a Distance*.

Upon our return from summer camp, dad immediately started expanding upon our homeschooling curriculum to include Spanish lessons. Dad had lived in Spain a couple times during the 1970's. He worked as a jazz pianist in several old casinos around Barcelona. Although he hadn't really spoken a lot of Spanish since then and was a bit rusty at it, he could certainly get the rest of the family started. We added an hour everyday to our homeschooling in which dad would gather us (including mom) into the living room and show us the basics of the language.

We started out with pronouns and basic present-tense conjugation. Conjugation in Spanish is a lot more specific than that of English and it was one of the hardest concepts to grasp. Once we learned that and started building a very small vocabulary of nouns (with their respective gender), tossed together with a few articles and prepositions, we were forming basic sentences. Dad used to test our comprehensive abilities by saying sentences which made no sense to see if we would catch them and laugh. "We have a blue car." "The squirrel has a blue car."...

And so it continued for many, many months. It was a new and interesting education dynamic, especially for mom who was used to playing the role of teacher, not student. We studied for the whole scholastic year leading up to our voyage and although we were by no means fluent upon our arrival in Spain, we certainly had a bit of a linguistic foundation. We were going through the necessary motions, but none of us had really processed what we were about to do. At this point, it was just a matter of going through the motions.

Other than Spanish lessons and preparation to rent out our home for a year, 2003 continued rather normally. Our friendships with the Adamses, Terrys, Garrisons, Simpsons,

McCormicks, and Grangers continued growing and adapting.

2003 was another example in the period of many, many years in which there was so much cross-influence between the Horsley family and the Adams family. Our families were so influenced and influential to each other that we were mimicking behaviors and choices, both big and small.

Many years prior, when we decided to get rid of the channels on our TV and use it solely for VHS tapes, the Adamses decided to place a limit of 30mins per day on their TV. Both families decided to join SPICE, the ethnic dancing group and for a long while we danced together. When Amy started playing lots of tennis with her dad, we were inspired to sign up for tennis lessons with Jennifer Dietrich. Years later, when we took up sailing, the Adamses joined.

We both had family dogs which loved playing together. We got our dogs around the same time and Amy and I got pet birds around the same time. Dolly and Sammy played a lot together. Apricot and Emerald were, well, birds. They chirped a lot together. Much of the extended family for both the Horsleys and the Adamses lived faraway and we celebrated most major holidays together. It was always far more than just a childhood friendship.

We always celebrated Halloween together. Some years during the Harry Potter craze (which Amy and I also shared), we dressed as witches. Other years we went as princesses. One year I dressed as a zombie cheerleader and Amy went as a gigantic soccer ball.

Throughout highschool, a Thanksgiving dinner between the two families became somewhat of a tradition. Even now that Amy and I can't always attend, our families still celebrate together and send us pictures of their festive shenanigans. It's still totally acceptable (and not unusual) for us to barge in unexpectedly to each other's homes.

Especially during childhood, there was always a huge deal made of our birthdays. Dad used to provide entertainment by playing games and singing songs, as usual. Amy's parents - Huey and Andy - were always very kind, warm-hearted and sometimes much more socially intuitive than my father, who had the tendency of getting a little caught up in festivities.

It always seemed to be the perfect mix of personalities. Dad was always pushing the boundaries, and while other people might be offended or embarrassed by that, the Adamses just laughed and played along. Not too long ago, Amy reminded me of one time when dad started speaking in a fake British accent to strangers and then discovered that they were *actually* British. Of course, there were far more ridiculous things that happened, from him insisting on singing all restaurant orders to dressing as the Pope to go grocery shopping.

One time, dad expressed an interest in Buddhism, Huey's religion. She was thrilled to teach him about it and we even attended a Buddhist event on the beach with Amy and her mom. It ended up in laughter though, when during a meditation, in the exact moment in which the leader said, "there is no poison in our lives", a snake appeared out of nowhere and started slithering across the floor. Amy and I couldn't keep straight faces.

The month of May inevitably arrived and we stuck to our plan. My birthday party that April was more of a going-away party with our closest friends. The church also threw us a little celebration and someone in the congregation went to the trouble of buying *rioja* for the event.

# Chapter 7:
## Spain 1

As I think back on all the eventful years in our childhood, there are some in which the memories seem to drift a bit. I can't seem to connect the event or the feeling thereof with its exact place in our history. I remember the many late-night, pool-deck conversations under the endless moon. I remember our sailing days of disciplining the wind and realizing how small the space is between the land and its sky. The memories come in waves - little bits of feelings and flickers in time. If there's any one year which stands out more than any other, it is 2004. It was the year in which everything and everyone changed.

When people ask me about it, it's very hard to condense the story into a reasonable time for a casual conversation. I must've told dozens of people by now about our biggest adventure, but I've never done the story justice. If anyone really wants to know about it, I tell them of the book my dad wrote about it. For here and now, I will try to condense things.

After many months of meeting with potential renters for our house and the protocol which accompanied this (making the beds, cleaning the floors, turning on all the lights, etc.), we finally found a man named Woody who seemed to be a good fit. He also agreed to maintain the pool while we were gone.

One morning - very early in the morning - we packed everything we could into 2 suitcases and a backpack each (the limit for most airlines). We hauled them out into the front yard and waited for our 5am taxi to Tampa International Airport. This memory - this one little memory of the four of us and our luggage waiting for the taxi - is the one dad returns to. It's the one time and place he wishes we could all return to and do all over again. It was the point at which we all embarked on our family's greatest adventure and at the time, none of us knew anything about it yet.

We were hardly even conscious when we arrived in Spain, in the Barajas Airport of Madrid. It was raining the day of our arrival, which made everything even more surreal and unclear. Despite our Spanish lessons at home, we were immediately humbled by how little we actually understood. Dad conducted all the necessary conversations and we collapsed in the Don Jaime hostel.

Our education began immediately. Dad finagled it so Jason and I could attend the last month or so of scholastic classes. (The school year in Europe runs until late June.) Jason was thrown into classes at Sagrado Corazon and I into Mariano Quintanilla. It was understood that we were auditing classes so we could get assimilated and learn Spanish in preparation for the upcoming scholastic year in which our grades would really matter. Dad also signed us up for a couple of summer activities after the school year ended. We both attended a theatre camp in a small town called Bejar, in the area of La Coruña. It was really hard to improvise a scene on stage in a foreign language!

Dad also hired a couple of tutors for us to speed up the process of language acquisition and academic success. Pedro Alvarez, our soon-to-be history professor, agreed to help us catch up. His son — I can't remember his name, but he looked like a bear — helped us out with our social studies, too. There was a young college student whose name I also can't remember, but she helped us with science.

And so it was. I was placed into "3 E.S.O" (freshman year) and Jason was placed into the equivalent of 6th grade.

We became extremely close friends with a girl named Gabriela Georgieva who was my age and lived with her family in a little apartment by the cathedral. There was a very special understanding between her and us which I  don't think we ever really discussed at the time. She had come to Spain because her homeland, Bulgaria, was in a very bad financial recession and her father could not find work. She was also thrown into a foreign country and a foreign language. Even though her reasons for moving to Spain and learning Spanish were very different than ours, she empathized with our difficulties. She was a great teacher as well as a great friend. She was always very patient with us, even when we couldn't be patient with ourselves and couldn't communicate something well.

Every morning, she rang our doorbell and we walked together through the hazy morning air and under the aqueduct's early glow, to school. Gabi and I sat together in class, passed endless little notes while the teachers lectured, walked home after school, made plans together for the evening. We were inseparable.

Jason was very young at this time and his friendships were perhaps more like those of children than the awkward teenager ones I was having. He goofed around with another boy named Marcos who he met at Sagrado Corazon. He also became friends with a brother and sister named Dino and Ase, who became very good friends with the whole family. Although they had come from a very troubled home and were perhaps ostracized by other kids at school because of it, their spirits were always very high and they were fun company.

We all lived in this beautiful duplex right on the Calle Real, which was one of the main streets in town, lined with little cafes and shops. We saw so many parades from our doorstep. The other side of the duplex faced a park four or five stories below. There was also a very vibrant discotheque - El Sabbat - which was in the park, directly under the windows of the master bedroom. Mom and dad got creative and built "aislantes" - huge, foamy insulation cushions cut to the exact dimensions of the windows. Our landlord, Valentin, was impressed.

Mom became close friends with a character named Justo, who used to sit at our dining table eating our chocolate and smoking cigarette after cigarette. He was a very sociable man, and very awkward. Although he could be a bit disgusting at times, wearing the same smudged green blazer every day, he was certainly a Spaniard who spoke nothing but Spanish and helped mom with the language while dad worked and we were at school.

Mom and dad also became good friends with a few ex-patriot couples and were constantly invited to social engagements throughout the city. There was an American woman who fell in love with a Spaniard and moved to Spain to live there with him. There was a crazy hippie lady named Julia who made jewelry and bathed in rivers naked. There was an ex-bullfighter who humored dad for a while. There were just so many characters.

Dad even finagled the rental of an upright piano for our duplex so we could continue practicing. For whatever reason, Jason and I got really interested in the music of Chopin during this time. We bought tons of etudes and ballades and were constantly playing through them while mom was in the kitchen, learning how to make an authentic "tortilla espanola".

When people ask, I tell them that Segovia was the best thing that happened to me. And it's the truth. Before that magical year in Spain, I was very socially inhibited. Despite my willingness to be on stage, I was probably a very socially awkward kid. I was homeschooled and sat in my room reading books for most of the day. I had a few friends, of course. Amy and Reguli were very close to me, but even my contact with them was probably less than normal.

In my observance of social growth from child to adult, I find that there is a very common age - somewhere around 14 - which is pivotal in terms of maturation. I've found it to be the case with most of my friends and it was certainly the case with me. As corny as it may sound, Segovia really made me into the person I am today. It was a year of personal exploration like none other. Everything was so condensed into that one year. It was the year everything happened. My first kiss, my first beer, my first cigarette, my first real school and social life - everything happened that year.

This was also the year when I first started listening to music that was not classical or jazz. Jason and I, in a way, discovered rock n' roll. And, in a way, it was an inevitability.

I'm not entirely sure what the trigger was, but both of us were at an impressionable time, especially me. Perhaps we were looking to relate with what we considered to be a minority, a special kind of kid whose music tastes affected how he or she dressed and acted. It's safe to say that in both the summer camps and at Quintanilla, the majority of kids were identified as "pijas" (the "preps"), a stereotype that was based around the emphasis of one's gender and its conformity therein. The boys were especially boyish - playing sports, congregating in groups, chatting about girls behind their backs. The girls dressed and acted their part, paying close attention to things like fashion and popularity. They also generally stuck together in gaggles and could easily be seen from afar as all having identical personalities.

Obviously, these stereotypes were exacerbated by the social tendencies of high school and the inherent desire to label one another. The preppy girls were not always superficial and girly. The preppy boys were not always sporty and immature. To us, though, they all appeared to be.

On the other hand, there was very obvious minority presence of those kids who instead embraced a more "alternative" appearance and personality. Whether self-identified as rocker, metalhead, punk, etc., they wore clothes which represented the music they listened to - something which had great affect on the personality and camaraderie with other like-minded teens.

The boys were not particularly boyish, often growing their hair out very long and wearing make-up. The girls were also not particularly girly. They rejected the concept of feminine style and instead embraced loosely-fitting clothes, dark colors, chains as bracelets, studs as accessories, etc. Ironically, it became a goal to fit in with this crowd which condemned the concept of conformity. But I especially wanted so badly to have an identity which was relatable, it just felt right.

The music was a determining factor as well. It was contagious and larger than life. It hit hard and made its point. Rock music was the greatest thing. The outward message of triumph through adversity, condemnation of societal norms, defiance of authority - all through cheesy lyrics (which perhaps weren't cheesy at the time) - all struck a certain chord in our impressionable, desperate minds. Mom and dad brushed it off, referring to our style and music choice as the "death and agony phase", but I really think there was so much more behind it. It's ridiculous and probably embarrassing looking back on it now and just how affected we were by that lifestyle. It was so important then.

It's interesting to note, however, that the two girls who became my closest friends identified otherwise. Although both were very close with the metalheads, the goths, the punks, etc., Gabi was much more into the hip hop movement and dressed accordingly. Bea dressed relatively preppy although she hung out a lot with the alternative groups. Despite our differences in style and identity, we acted like peas in a pod, inseparable friends throughout freshman year.

Jason was intrigued by this new outlook and started listening to the same music I did. We both became obsessed with the music of Metallica, Iron Maiden, Black Sabbath, A.F.I, Blink-182, Slipknot... It really did become an obsession. We'd spend days deciding which new CD we would buy when we had the money. We'd spend any leftover change on rock n' roll magazines at the street kiosks. We cut out pictures of our favorite bands and started taping them to our walls, our notebooks, anything to publicly display our tastes, in hopes that kids with similar preferences would identify with us.

And they did! We were also quickly introduced to rock bands of Spain. We began listening to Mago de Oz, Lujuria, and Ska-P. Carlos ("Lechon") who was also in my grade started burning me mix after mix from his personal music collection and informing me of local shows. I always had a bit of a crush on him because of his seemingly fearless extroversion around the other kids and his contagious enthusiasm about music.

Dad and mom had their own social outlets. Dad started meeting local musicians almost immediately and was able to join a big band ensemble called *Let The Children Play*. He also did smaller collaborations with some of its participants like Cris, the drummer, and Parra, the bassist. For mom, everything was an educational experience. Even buying fruit at the market required the language! Despite their little quirks, Justo and Gustavo were good friends who were more than willing to help when they could to develop her Spanish skills. She took vigorous notes and studied every night.

Mom and dad would go with the ex-pats or the band or the parents of our friends or any number of different people on the weekends while Jason and I had our own plans. My evenings usually went the latest because of my age - we'd end up in Los Zulus or El Salon until the wee hours of the night, sharing calimochos (gross mixed drinks of Coca-Cola and boxed wine) and talking about bands or boys.

I had a little crush on a kid named Jorge Vegas, but it never really amounted to anything other than holding hands. I remember being frustrated the night I wanted to kiss him because he had a sore throat and didn't want to give it to me. I should have been flattered.

My first kiss was with a boy named Manuel Jimenez Martin (*"Manu"*) on December 1st, 2004. He was a year older than me and belonged to our group of friends. From our 3E.S.O classrooms on the second floor, we used to sit on the steps and try to guess which feet belonged to which kid on the third floor, where the 5E.S.O classrooms were.

Anyway, Manu was a very sweet kid and he was wicked smart. He was one of the quieter boys who usually kept his feelings to himself. He offered to help me with my physics homework one day, since I was really having a hard time understanding it. (He later went on to pursue physics at the university level and is now doing his Master's thesis in it.) He came over to our apartment and it was super awkward because we both liked each other but were too scared to say anything about it.

I offered to accompany him to his bus stop. As we left the apartment, it started raining torrentially and everyone fled from the streets. We ducked under the awning of a closed store and then ran down the stairs into the Parque Salon, only to discover that he had missed his bus and we had a little while to wait before the next one would come.

We told me he wanted to show me one of his favorites spots of the city, which wasn't that far away. He took me to a little alleyway, hidden among old buildings and narrow cobblestone streets. It was behind the main Calle Real and it tunneled behind the cathedral. It was still drizzly out and the streets were empty. We spent a few endless minutes giggling and trying to stammer out words. We inched ourselves closer and closer. After a long silence broken up only by our embarrassed chuckles and short bursts of eye contact, I put my hands on his shoulders and said, *"me atrevo o no me atrevo?"* (Do I dare or do I not?) *"Atrevete"* (I dare you), he said and pulled me into him. It was horribly awkward, of course; a first kiss for both of us. But it was beautiful. It was memorable. I wouldn't have had it any other way.

And so it was. He and I "dated" for the rest of the time that I was in Spain. We'd meet under a certain arch of the aqueduct during recess to giggle and make out, away from our friends. We'd hold hands in the hallways, even if we were just walking a few steps. It was sweet. We were crazy about each other.

There were so many other memorable moments during that autumn semester. There was the time the whole family went to see Lujuria in a gymnasium of a nearby town. The band was from Segovia originally - the crazy, tattooed lead singer, nicknamed "El Oso" (the bear) used to teach preschool down the street from us. Before the show, we met the keyboardist, Nuria, and introduced ourselves as a family. During the show, in front of all my closest friends and thousands of other screaming fans, the band mentioned us on stage and dedicated a song to me. At the time, I considered it to be one of the greatest moments of my life.

There are so, so many other things I should mention, but a book about this has already been written. I should mention the crazy fiestas de San Lorenzo, our visit to a remote village in the Pyrenees mountains where we went skiing and where dad also considered living, the spontaneous Christmas trip to London and spilling hot chocolate on myself on Christmas morning in some random pub, the time when Josh Terry and his mother visited us, the time I danced on the bar at Sabbat, the frequent trips to La Granja, the ridiculous parade of the devil at the aqueduct, Titirimundi (the festival of puppets which involved people wearing huge paper-mache masks and wacking random people on the street with brooms), the time I sang Tower of

Power songs with dad's funk band, the innumerable evenings that started at 6pm and ended at 2am with everything in between...

After even a few months, Jason and I were completely fluent and I made a huge effort to lose any trace of an accent when speaking. Ironically, Segovia became more of a home than St. Petersburg, FL ever was. It seemed like we all had everything there (apartment, school, music, social lives, etc.) and it was crazy to even think of ever going back to America.

But, as all things eventually come to an end, Segovia was no exception.

There were issues on the horizon that we needed to tend to and although we wanted to stay in Segovia for the entire year, we had to cut it 2 months short. Of our entire childhood, this is the only thing dad claims to regret. Of course, we knew far less about what was on the other side of the Atlantic Ocean waiting for us than we did about the town in Spain with which we had fallen in love.

We had two very teary goodbye parties (one for the adults and the other for the kids). Gabi tried to convince us to stay over and over again. There were so many things we had yet to experience there. I never got to celebrate my birthday there, nor were we able to finish the scholastic year (and prove that we were able to pass all our classes - which we were doing!). Our neighbor - the mayor's mother - gave us a lovely little statue of the patron saint of Segovia upon hearing that we were leaving. My friends all signed a t-shirt, which I'm terrified of washing to this day. It all happened quite suddenly and none of us really had time to process what we were leaving. We ended up right back under the aqueduct with two suitcases and a backpack each in the early hours of the morning, now knowing what exactly what Segovia was. On the airplane back, when the stewardesses started speaking in perfect English, we all felt very strange and out-of-place. Was this reality? Did Segovia even happen?

# Chapter 8:
## Return to the U.S.A

All I can tell on paper are the facts as they could fit in one of grandpa's macadamia nutshells. This saga is one that should really be told late at night around the pool with a glass of wine or something stronger.

As the story goes, we cut our year in Spain to ten months so we could help grandma move closer to us. It was a very difficult decision to make and neither option was desirable. We were all devastated to leave Spain. We threw two epic parties before we left, one for adults and one for kids. Dad passed around a book and, by the end of each party, it was filled with signatures and drawings we still cherish today.

We had rented our house out for the complete year and so when we returned after only 10 months, we had nowhere to stay. We ended up renting a dumpy little apartment by the old Gateway Mall, living on plastic lawn furniture and feeling even more out of place in what was technically our home town. Even our friends had grown a bit apart in the time that we had been gone. We came back "home" to practically nothing.

To make matters worse, grandma started being extremely fickle with her plans. Things went back and forth between her and my father, trying to decide where she would be happiest and how we could facilitate that for her. After many difficult conversations, grandma and dad decided to split the cost of the house directly adjacent to ours in Meadowlawn. The day after they signed the contract, grandma reneged on the deal and my dad decided that he had had enough of her indecision.

Jason and I still had our minds on Spain. American School felt so weird; it was odd to just be another American kid like everyone else. We anxiously awaited the boxes of Quintanilla textbooks and notebooks we had shipped home. When the boxes arrived at the post office, however, we were greeted with the ripped remains of cardboard, packing peanuts, strangely, rip-off Playboy magazines. Losing our books was devastating, but we've often joked how much worse it was for that other guy must have been when our foreign textbooks arrived.

It's hard to remember exactly when and how many times Jason and I transferred schools. Jason finished middle school at Meadowlawn, but transferred several times before finding a good fit for high school. I finished my freshman year at the PCCA (arts) program at Gibbs before realizing that, although the music program was encouraging, the academics were laughable. Even among the music students, I did not fit in. I was terrified to be seen alone in the cafeteria, so many times I hid in the bathroom stall like a loser and snarfed down some crackers where I wouldn't be seen. I did make friends with two very troubled teenagers while in the program. Craig was a lanky gay boy who was constantly suffering from Diet Coke addiction migraines and getting in trouble for stealing his mom's pain meds. Rhia came from a very broken family and toyed around with cutting, which I didn't really understand at the time.

One day, she pulled up her pant leg and showed me a little heart that she had carved into her knee like a tattoo. I thought it looked kinda pretty so I tried to do it to myself. I really quickly realized that it was very painful and stupid, but I couldn't help her see that. I'm not sure why I was attracted to these two kids. I guess it's because they were self-identified as alternative and into the same kind of music that I was. It was by no means the healthy social environment that I had in Spain.

For the beginning of my sophomore year, Amy convinced me to transfer to St. Petersburg High's International Baccalaureate program, which is where she was attending. It's important to note, however, that the past year had changed us in very different ways. I was completely enveloped in the rocker/metal culture and she had become affected by the academic/girly crowd at SPHS, which - of course- was the polar opposite, in high school culture.

Ironically, the International Baccalaureate did not accept my credits from Spain and required me to double up on math and science. This left me no electives and no free time to study music in the evenings. It was not a good match. I may or may not have pulled out to join the regular (not IB) program at SPHS, but it became very quickly apparent that there was a negative divide among the students between IB or "regular".

All aside, I did have a very positive experience in meeting two of Amy's friends, Matt Moench and John Paul, who were both excellent musicians and were starting a band. I became their keyboardist and we played together for over a year. We had very few actual gigs - the only one I remember distinctly was for the Jewish temple in Pasadena in which one of the rabbis was generous with both offering and consuming wine, leading to him dancing on top of tables and us playing Hava Nagila way too many times because it was the only Jewish song we knew.

We had lots of great experimental jam sessions, however, and even though we all pretty much sucked at improvising at that age, there was potential and only one way to get good at it. I remember sometimes we would lay down rules: we made promises to not use any words to express ourselves for specific periods of time (an hour, two hours...), so we were forced to improvise, uninterrupted. It was great fun and I loved hanging out with those guys.

After PCCA, IB and SPHS, I gave up on finding a decent high school. There was a program at Saint Petersburg College which was popular among homeschoolers that seemed to be the best option. It was called St. Petersburg Collegiate High School and basically involved high school-aged kids dual-enrolling in college-level classes which would ultimately count for both high school and college credit. The idea was to graduate high school with an AA (Associate's Degree), which was roughly 60 credits and the equivalent of 2 years in full-time college enrollment.

For the summer of 2005, we invited the twins Clara and Paula, two girls who went to high school with us in Segovia, to visit us in Florida. Although they weren't very close friends with us at the time, they came from a relatively affluent family and it was not financially difficult for them to make the trip. We were desperate for the opportunity to experience Segovia again, even if it was just a very little bit of it coming to us.

Their visit ended up actually being comically disastrous. The twins had already been to America and were therefore relatively unimpressed by many of the things we were excited to show them. It was great to speak in pure Castilian Spanish again, but it wasn't worth the ungrateful attitudes.

One very memorable moment of their visit was when we introduced them to Eddy, our neighbor. Eddy was a very friendly, uneducated man whose profession was trimming trees. His language reflected his education level and the interaction between him and the Spanish girls was very comical. Clara and Paula had studied English for many years and considered themselves fluent until this one conversation. After we explained to Eddy that they were from Spain, he hollered, "Aw! You's a ways away, ain'tcha?". The look on their faces upon hearing this kind of English was priceless.

It was also during this time that dad took a position at Trinity United Church of Christ, working with Pastor Robert Palin. He was a very academic man whose sermons rarely got through to the common folk who attended. He was not, however, controlling or arrogant. He was a pleasant man to work alongside and he appreciated the music we provided. Jason and I kept studying the organ there and would frequently have long Sunday afternoon practice sessions which sometimes involved taking breaks to order pizza and eat it on the altar. Trinity UCC was also on the way to SPC and therefore an easy commute from classes.

At the time, Jason and I were still very much into rock music and Jason's interest in video games was growing more and more. We looked forward to Warped Tour months in advance and knew the concert schedule for Jannus Landing by heart. We'd go downtown and hang out at our old stomping grounds - Fortunato's, Moon under Water, etc. We began frequenting a hipster coffee shop close to Mirror Lake called The Globe. Dad helped us sneak through the backs of restaurants and alleyways into shows at Jannus since they were so expensive. It was more fun to sneak into them anyway. Sometimes we'd go to elaborate measures to sneak in, only to leave after deciding that we hated the band.

Like most dumb and overly self-conscious teenagers, I was mortified to be seen with my dad and little brother, even though I always had infinitely more fun hanging out with them than any of my friends. I remember going to an Avenged Sevenfold show one time when I was trying so hard to be cool and hardcore in front of some punk friends (whose acceptance I so desperately wanted). Dad was with me and I tried to pretend that I wasn't actually with him. I pushed my way to the other side of the crowd as to not be seen with my father.

A few songs into the first set, one of the punks tapped me on the shoulder and yelled, "Dude! Your dad is outside with some paramedics! So hardcore!". Apparently, someone was crowdsurfing in front of my dad (who was so cool and had gotten much closer to the stage than I was) and someone's head bumped into my dad's, causing a pretty serious nosebleed. I scrambled outside and, sure enough, there was dad, laughing and holding a bloody tissue to his face.

Another time when dad accompanied us to Warped Tour on an impossibly hot day in August, he caused a hilarious scene by approaching a lady who was selling water bottles for $4 and paying her to sit in her huge bucket of ice.

And another time, when we attended the much-anticipated Hoobastank show at Jannus, dad took me - all jittery after the concert - to the adjacent restaurant where we ended up meeting the band itself while they were playing billiards! Things were always just so much more interesting with dad around and it took me forever to appreciate it. From dancing in mosh pits to wearing dresses in public, dad was always the life of the party.

Jason started taking karate lessons with Joey (who now requested to be called "Joe") at Superkicks on 9th Street. He got really good and although I joined a year or so later, I never reached his level. He and Joe were still very close friends and they got together often to play video games.

It was also around this time that I started taping concert tickets and movie stubs to my wall. Little did I know at the time, but this was the beginning of my obsessive Wall of Life.

It was in 2005 that I also got my first solo gig at a church. Allendale United Methodist hired me (for peanuts) to be their organist and choir accompanist. They had a little 20-rank Zimmer at the far wall of the church and although it was a small position, it was very satisfying to have my own gig.

Eventually we had to say goodbye to the nice people of Trinity UCC as they got a new pastor and dad decided he'd rather work somewhere else. We found a motion-activated music box which we left in the toilet paper roll of his bathroom, making the party very eventful when anyone used the facilities and was quickly surprised by music coming from the toilet paper roll. Typical Horsley prank.

I toyed with the idea of working for a black gospel church called New Hope Missionary Baptist Church, but they couldn't pay anything and, although very entertaining, it would've been a big time commitment.

Things were going very well for me at SPC. Dad encouraged me to join not only the college choir, but also the select vocal ensemble called Madrigalians, under the direction of Dr. Vernon Taranto ("Dr. T"). I was scared to death of the audition, but dad accompanied me and I got in immediately. That ensemble ended up becoming my closest group of friends and I thoroughly enjoyed making music with Dr. T.

I got my learner's license (like Amy) when I was 15 and was required to keep a log book of my driving experience. Dad gave me my first driving lessons in the parking lot of Derby Lane, the horse and dog racing track by Gandy Beach. A few times as kids we had taken field trips there to do math and calculate how much every gambler would probably lose. Anyway, the homeschooling never really stopped. Dad started teaching me both organ and driving lessons daily.

Exactly a year later, right around my 16th birthday, I got my driver's license. After many exhausting days of shopping around for a car, I fell in love with Lucille, a 2000 Pontiac Bonneville SLE. Dad dickered on the price and we bought it. I was so thrilled. Amy also got a car - a white Kia Optima - and was equally excited about this new and incredible freedom.

Jason and I started playing at a little neighborhood church a block away from our house called Grace Community Baptist Church. Despite the pastor being racist and dumb and preaching sermons condemning "evil-ution", the convenience of a practice organ was convincing enough, at least for a little while. One day when my friend Craig was spending the night, I invited him to come with me to the church late at night so I could play something for him. We had keys, naturally, and I didn't hesitate to pull on the full organ to play a big Bach fugue.

As we walked back home that night, we were suddenly greeted by 3 cop cars behind us - lights, sirens and all. A neighbor who saw the two of us enter the church - in all black and obviously teenagers - got frightened, thinking that the church was being broken into. I tried to explain that I was the organist, but the cops wouldn't have any of it. I called home and told mom to not freak out but that there were cops who wanted to talk to her. She was totally cool and explained to the officers  that I was, in fact, an organist. They let us go. Poor Craig was completely spooked. He was underage and had a pack of cigarettes on him - wide-eyed whining for the rest of the night about how he could have gone to jail, yadda yadda.

At the time, I was "dating" this boy named Alex Patch, who I had actually met at Friends Music Camp (before we left for Spain). For whatever reason, we began chatting online and hit it off really well. Now that I look back on it, I think the biggest reason why I was with him was because I was so desperately trying to be older and be taken more seriously. Having a boyfriend supposedly catapulted oneself into the world of adulthood, which I was so eager to join, especially being surrounded by college-age kids at SPC. Throughout the entire relationship, we saw each other only twice. He visited me in Florida and then I visited him once in New Orleans, when he was staying there with his family. Despite his obvious and uncomfortable disagreements with his parents, I had a really lovely time.

It took me way too long, but I finally came to my senses and realized that he was just an insecure, immature boy and I was just being needy and looking for an excuse to have a boyfriend. We were young, desperately trying to feel needed and understood. It was fun at the time, but I'm glad I got it out of my system.

By this time, we had all finally re-assimilated into the normalcy of American life. Amy and I were driving back and forth to school, Jason was finishing middle school and enjoying video games with Joe, mom was back to work as an RN with Baycare, dad kept working for Metro (which was now called Advanced Assessments). Things with grandma had finally settled, as best as they could (which was not very well at all) and both Jason and I seemed to have found a school which was working for us, at least for the time being.

There was always, however, an itch in all of us for another big adventure. Spain was now very expensive, with the Euro being strong, but there were many other places in the world that spoke Spanish which we had yet to discover.

For the summer of 2006, we moved to Guanajuato, Mexico.

# Chapter 9:
# Guanajuato, Mexico

Immediately after concluding my sophomore year at SPC and Jason's last year of middle school, we moved to a little town about 7 hours north of Mexico City called Guanajuato. I remember the long day of travel to get to Mexico. Even though it appeared to just be on the other side of the Gulf of Mexico, it was indeed a very faraway place. As soon as we arrived in Mexico City, we took a grueling Flecha Amarilla bus from there all the way to Guanajuato, passing through the impoverished outskirts of the capital to vast deserts to remote mountain pueblos and everything in between.

Arriving in Guanajuato was a magical experience. A taxi from the bus station took us to the center of the city. After he dropped us off, we had to walk up a flight of stairs, with no idea what we would expect to see at the top. Lo and behold, we were greeted by the most beautiful, lively town square (El Jardin Principal), where outdoor restaurants were bustling with people and several mariachi bands in full regalia were all playing at the same time, trumpets wailing, old couples dancing among the flowerbeds, little kids running around with ice cream cones, flocks of teenage girls full of giggles and swishy skirts. It was the kind of life that we had only previously equated with Europe - the very outdoor culture, people of all ages in the streets mingling and socializing. There was life everywhere.

After several days of calling rental listings in Mil Cosas, we ultimately decided to just take to the streets and ask people face to face, randomly, if they happened to know of anybody who was renting. We finally found a good match when we stumbled upon a nice restaurant by the university called El Tapatio. The owner said that his family regularly rented out to traveling students and would be willing to make accommodations for us.

Guadalupe's house was on the rim of the bowl which was the city. Essentially, the town was built into a ravine, surrounded by mountains. The panoramic highway (La Panoramica) circled the town along the edge of the mountains. It had a beautiful view of the city and was a healthy 300 steps (of various shapes and sizes) down. The deal was that we paid a certain amount every month in rent and that this money also covered our meals which we could either eat at home with Guadalupe or in the city at her husband's restaurant.

Jason and I were once again thrown into the last few weeks of a random high school in a foreign country. After much discussion and casual jokes with the principal, dad was granted an exception which allowed Jason and me to attend for the rest of their scholastic year. The name of the school was LaSalle and it was a Catholic school in the city. We had to wear dorky uniforms and everyday dad walked us down to the bus station.

The students were generally nice and welcoming, but there were definitely social cliques which were established and it was obvious that we didn't fit in. It's an odd feeling as an American to be the minority in a country like Mexico. Tables turned.

We quickly found other activities to augment and expand our social lives. We began attending salsa classes and singing in a choir at the town's big basilica under the direction of Francisco, an adorable alcoholic and neurotic perfectionist. Dad and I had never sung chant in a choir and it was a really awesome experience. I think I also sang a short solo for a concert we put on. Anyway, Francisco would go out for drinks

after every rehearsal and order an entire bucket of beers just for himself. Mom and dad were understandably concerned about his health, but at least there wasn't driving involved (the town was very European in that everyone walked or took public transit) and he was an innocent drunk who just babbled about classical music.

One time, after a successful performance, he invited the entire choir to his apartment where everybody was expected to bring a dish. One of the oldest, daintiest sopranos brought chips and homemade salsa which was the spiciest thing dad had ever tasted in his whole life. We laughed about that for a good while.

We also frequented a bar called Zilch which was known for having great live jazz. The city of Guanajuato was very culturally vibrant and hosted a massive jazz festival every year that brought in all the biggest names. There were also the faithful "estudiantines," which were essentially university students who celebrated their Mexican heritage by parading through the streets every Thursday, Friday, and Saturday night playing traditional instruments, singing songs and generally making a huge scene. They were always trailed by a hundred locals on any given day, all singing along and drinking out of traditional frog-shaped pitchers. ("Guanajuato" apparently meant something like "pile of frogs" in the indigenous language).

Occasionally, we'd take little day trips to nearby towns like San Miguel de Allende or just to get out into nature and ride ATVs around the mountains. There were plenty of things within the city of Guanajuato, however, to keep us thoroughly entertained. Jason and I tagged along with mom when she went to the big Mercado Hidalgo to go shopping. Going anywhere (especially somewhere like the Mercado Hidalgo) was a completely overwhelming sensory experience. People were shouting and singing and peddling goods, little kids ran around barefoot, vibrant colors were everywhere, the smell of some strange meat wafted from a street vendor, the ground was filthy and you had to wash a layer of dust off your legs at the end of the day. People were born here and spent their entire lives here.

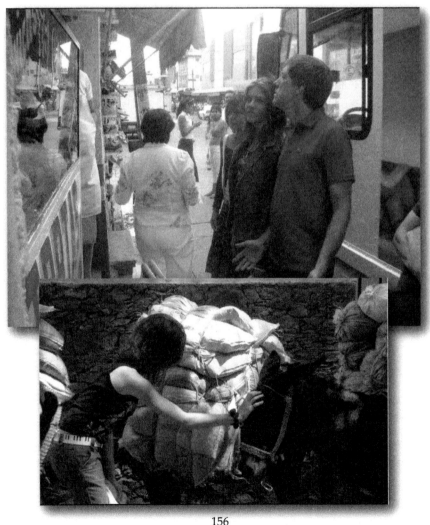

The town was very well-known for its silver mines, which were still in use. A large portion of the population was still employed as miners, which was still a very dangerous way to make a living. Nevertheless, the city produced beautiful silver jewelry for unbelievable prices. Mom and I bought quite a few beautiful amulets during our time there - mostly of the Aztec calendar, plated with various indigenous stones. Every time I see an Aztec design, I think of the silver jewelry of Guanajuato.

There were also the "momias" which we didn't find to be as appealing as other cultural activities. But yes, there was a collection of mummies that brought in many tourists. Much in line with the Mexican culture, there was a strange sort of cultural comfort with death. I'm not just referring to Dia de los Muertos, which is the festival everyone associates with Mexico. The Mexicans are notoriously

Catholic and superstitious. They spoke of death often and casually. It was odd for an American to observe this.

Since Jason was still very obsessed with his video games, dad was constantly looking for a way to get him outside more often and involved in the Mexican culture. He found a beautiful Mexican college student who offered to show him around the city as a tour guide of sorts. Dad gladly paid for their tickets into museums and concerts. It was the source of many jokes that Jason, a little 14-year-old kid was being escorted around the city by a very beautiful native. Sometimes I would tag along with and enjoy the field trips. One time we visited a haunted house and I swear to God there was an actual dead body inside.

Life in Mexico was ridiculously cheap on all levels. In contrast to Spain's euro, the Mexican peso was very weak against the dollar. Jason and I would go to the movies for the equivalent of about $1 each. A really nice meal of several courses would add up to about $5. It was hard to leave a place where one could enjoy life on such a small budget!

For special occasions, we'd go somewhere fancy like El Rincon Gaucho, but even that wasn't anywhere near as expensive as any of the fancier restaurants back in St. Petersburg.

All in all, it was a fascinating experience. As Americans, we tend to think of Mexico as being a "third-world" country, but during our time there we discovered that in many ways it was the USA that was third-world. The town we lived in had a thriving cultural scene, with more live music on a regular basis than we had ever experienced in the huge metropolitan area of Tampa Bay.

Even the small town of Guanajuato had its own professional symphony - while Tampa is struggling to keep theirs! On one of our first nights there, we attended their performance of Tchaikovsky's 5th Symphony and I would have never expected to be so moved by the symphonic performance of a Russian composer in a remote Mexican town. It was stunning! The town also was known for its major university which is acknowledged internationally as an academic mecca. The natives were lovely, friendly people who were proud of their heritage and so very welcoming to anyone who showed an interest in their culture. We met so many fascinating people and had some incredible times - another amazing adventure for the Horsley family.

# Chapter 10:
# The Unheard Voice/Costa Rica

Upon our return to the United States, we all picked up where we had left off. Mom returned to the Baycare mobile pool, where she was called every other morning at some ungodly hour and told which area hospital she would be serving. Dad continued writing software and working for Josh Powe. He was always on the lookout for new and better church positions. Dad also enjoyed playing with Lee Ahlin for some of the productions at Shorecrest, a preparatory school which put on elaborate musicals every year. I went back to SPC and continued singing with Madrigalians and taking the necessary courses to complete my Associate's degree. Jason was now entering high school and had found a special program (TODD) at our zoned school, Northeast High, for students with advanced math/science skills.

At SPC, I had recently finished a literature course with a professor by the name of Linda LaPointe who was very inspiring for me. One day I remember she asked us to bring in a song which reminded us of poetry. It could be any genre or any instrumentation. She said that music was the closest relative to poetry and she wanted us to share our thoughts on that. Other times when it was obvious that the class was lacking inspiration, she used to throw her arms up in the air and exclaim, "Oh, just take 5 minutes. Go outside and sit under a tree. Look at the leaves and the grass and think about your existence. I'm serious! Get out! Do it!". And so we did. One day toward the end of the semester, she mentioned the fact that the college did not have a student publication. Had that thought even crossed our minds? Why didn't we have one? She told us that it was a great shame that students did not have a voice or a place to publish their thoughts. I couldn't agree more.

As the day went on and I went about my normal schedule, I couldn't stop thinking about her remarks that morning. For whatever reason, it really bothered me. The more I thought about it, the more it bothered me. I just couldn't shake it. That night, I wrote up a flyer asking for other students to join me in forming a newspaper. I printed 300 copies, and the very next morning at 6AM, I covered the campus with them.

LaPointe couldn't have been more thrilled. As the day progressed, I got call after call about my poster. By the end of the day I had acquired a group of passionate students who wanted to help out. Lisa Fountain, a girl I used to dance with in SPICE, was very interested in writing columns. Chris, a student in his 30's who was coming back for his degree, had significant experience in newspaper design and offered to help with layout. There were many others who were strong writers and excited about the idea of publishing. Professor LaPointe offered to write us blank checks for however much the printing cost.

Within a month, we had assembled our first issue. We called the newspaper *The Unheard Voice.* The first issue came out on my birthday. I remember sitting at Sir Speedy's Printing a few days prior, watching the machine churn out hundreds of copies of this newspaper with my name listed as the editor; it was a great feeling.

Its distribution turned quite a few heads, including that of my high school principal, Mrs. Linda Benware, and the college president, Karl Kutler. Not long after we distributed the first issue, I received an intimidating call from the president's attorney, asking for a meeting. Basically, the university was terrified that I would print something negative about administration and although I had plenty of material to do so, I never intended to publish anything negative. They claimed that my newspaper breached legalities and Mrs. Benware, in all her professional tact, said she could've had me "beheaded" for such behavior. Dad stood up for me and we got out relatively unscathed. The voice continued to be heard.

After consulting with a student law expert, I re-worded our disclaimer and continued publishing. I also quickly pulled out of Benware's collegiate high school program (and from under her oppressive thumb). Although all of my education was being done at SPC, mom claimed to be homeschooling me and enrolling me there as a dual-enrolled student. (It was a bit of a fudge, but it was acceptable to the state of FL and it went by unquestioned.) I continued publishing *The Unheard Voice.*

As spring came and ideas for summer travel started forming, we couldn't shake the thought of going somewhere new; somewhere none of us had ever been. Central America had a lot of intrigue. Since we all spoke Spanish, we could go almost anywhere in Central or South America and be understood. We could easily rule out a few countries which still had reputations of kidnappings and drug trafficking. Panama might be too touristic; Nicaragua was suffering from deforestation and the selling of endangered species on the black market.

Costa Rica seemed to be everything we were looking for. It was rustic and safe and affordable. The natives seemed American-friendly, while there were plenty of opportunities to escape from tourism. We booked a flight to San Jose, with the intention of exploring this new and fascinating country for a couple weeks.

It's important to note that there's only one major highway which runs through Costa Rica and it runs vertically, North-South. In order to cross from East to West or vice versa, there is nothing more than endless dirt roads through the rain forests. Coincidentally, that happened to be the exact direction which we were traveling. To make things more difficult, the vast majority of vehicles in the country were manual transmission.

Naturally, the rustic roads, winding around mountains and through massive forests, were a bit nauseating as a passenger. The solution was to drive instead and focus all mental energy on the road ahead. I had only recently gotten my driver's license and had spent many hours behind the wheel of my Bonneville, but that was automatic transmission. I was clueless when it came to driving a stick-shift car. Dad tried to teach me, if only to prevent my constant and inconvenient nausea attacks along the drive. I tried to be patient and learn, but it's hard to concentrate on something when your stomach is churning. It proved relatively unsuccessful, so Jason and dad just tried driving as smoothly as possible to compensate.

While in Costa Rica, we had pretty much every adventurous experience available. We did white-water rafting, zip-lined through layers of the rain forests, hiked up and down mountains, swam in swirling waterfalls, drove up volcanoes... We embraced every crazy opportunity and took pictures of our terrifying exploits. It was grand!

The country of Costa Rica has a national motto of sorts which can be found all over from government buildings to t-shirts. It's "Pura Vida" which literally translates to "pure life", although perhaps a more appropriate meaning would be something like, "full of life" or "this is living!". There is certainly no question about the lack of life in the country. Every direction you look is teeming with exotic forests, wild animals you would only otherwise see in zoos, stunning cliffs and volcanoes and waterfalls, enough adventures to satisfy Indiana Jones himself.

During one of our days of driving, as we circled the highest layer of the rain forest, we suddenly began hearing loud shrieking from the side of the road. We were all pretty taken aback by this with no idea what the sound could be attributed to. It sounded like children screaming. As we cautiously exited the car, we saw rustling in the forest and realized that it was actually an aggressive group of monkeys, perhaps fighting or making territorial claims. It was incredible. We wondered if they could possibly be violent to humans. We got back in the car and kept driving.

One of the places we stayed during our travels through Costa Rica was a place called Arenal Paraiso, named after the Arenal volcano. We lived in a log cabin of sorts and the property was covered in tiers of hot springs and natural pools. Bars had even been built in the hot springs so you could swim around and drink at the same time - no bar stools were really needed. One night we heard another loud sound which we couldn't recognize, emanating from the volcano. The natives told us not to worry; the volcano spits out huge fireballs all the time. We couldn't believe that they were serious, so like idiots we drove the rental car closer to the volcano itself to see for ourselves.

From the base of the mountain it was pretty clear. There were definitely huge molten rocks being spit from the mouth of the volcano and tumbling violently down the side, leaving behind trails of lava and fire. The volcano was very much active. We couldn't believe our eyes.

When we finally arrived on the Pacific coast of the country, we made arrangements to stay at another bizarre hotel/hostel of sorts which basically consisted of tree houses built into the upper layers of the rainforest and tethered together with dozens of little suspension bridges. The place was known for having a consistently higher population of monkey guests than humans throughout the year.

From our tree house, the ground level of the forest was nowhere within sight. We had no way of calculating exactly how high up we were in the forest, because each level was so densely populated by thick vegetation and animals. The rain forest is huge and intimidating place to be which really puts our human existence into perspective. We were far outnumbered by other intelligent species. One morning, we woke up in our tree house to find an uninvited guest on our deck. A humongous lizard, probably 3 feet in length, had decided to crawl up and hang out with us. We decided to let him stay. (We wouldn't have known how to move him anyway.)

After one of our hikes through the forest, as we were undressing back at the tree house, mom noticed a line of hard black dots around the ankle seams of our pants. They were fastened on tight and appeared to be some sort of decorative studs which we had not previously noticed when we bought them. Upon further examination and much to our terrified amazement, we realized that they were actually the heads of jungle ants which had bitten our pants and not let go. The jaws of these huge ants were so powerful that once they clamped on to something, the rest of their bodies would fall off before they would decide to let go. In primitive days, these ants were used as stitches, since they would so reliably bind things with their jaws. Come to think of it, I'm not sure we ever did get them off our pants.

We spent several days at the national park called Manuel Antonio, which stretches up and down the coast for miles. The sand on the beach was pitch black, which was a very beautiful and unusual sight. The monkeys around the beach had no fear of humans and would follow us around and jump out onto the trail with no hesitations. It was bizarre and amazing.

One of our favorite findings on the Pacific coast was a restaurant we stumbled across which was actually inside an old gutted airplane. To our surprise, the plane was one of the mysterious vehicles associated with the Iran Hostage Crisis which had made its way into Costa Rican territory and which the USA refused to claim responsibility for. The Costa Rican authorities decided to make it instead into a unique restaurant. As American

tourists, it was certainly an amusing reminder of our political reputation. Dad and Jason especially found this to be a very entertaining discussion with the natives.

By far the most memorable experience of our entire trip was the day we had to do laundry. With day after day of jungle hikes, zip-lining, etc., you can only imagine how filthy our clothes became. Doing laundry became an emergency of sorts. Our clothes were catastrophically dirty.

It must have been a Sunday or a holiday because very few places were open that day. We drove past town after town along the Pacific coast, asking in each little village for a laundromat, yielding no success.

Finally we decided to stop in one of the random little towns and just walk around. Perhaps we would have more luck on foot, asking any person in the street for help. Sure enough, we ended up finding a little hole-in-the-wall laundry room which was operated by a poor woman and her young daughter. She worked as a maid, doing laundry and other chores for a few of the more affluent (but still by no means wealthy) locals. She said that she could help us out but that our clothes would take a couple hours to clean since she only had a few machines. We thanked her graciously for accommodating our laundry needs and told her that the wait would not be a problem at all.

As she bent down to pick up our clothes and put them in one of the machines, mom noticed a huge wound on her leg. The woman confessed that she had been bitten by a spider in her sleep and it had gotten badly infected. (Keep in mind, of course, that Costa Rican spiders - like any other native species - are a hundred times more exotic and dangerous.) Mom explained that she was a nurse and she asked to see it up close.

The wound was nothing to be easily dismissed. The infection was the size of a golf ball, all covered in different bulging purples and reds, with little fingers of blood at its corners. There was one spot in which it was possible that the bone was visibly exposed. She had no money to see a doctor and she had no medical knowledge of her own. Mom told us that she would stay and help her while we went for a walk around the town, waiting for our laundry.

I can't remember exactly, but I think mom took her to a little clinic and bought her the drugs and care she needed. Although she couldn't afford it, healthcare in Central America was extremely affordable in comparison to ours in the USA. In the meanwhile, the rest of us decided it might be nice to buy her daughter something. She patiently waited while her mother worked, entertaining herself by making drawings. She only had a couple old pens and they didn't write very well. We bought her a nice set of colors for her drawings and a couple pads of sketch paper.

The girl's name was Hilary - an odd name for a Latin American girl. We commented that the 2008 elections for our country were on the horizon and that - at the time - it was possible for a woman named Hilary to become president. The girls eyes lit up.

Hilary was thrilled about her new art supplies and immediately drew her first piece - two princesses and their farms. She told me that we were the princesses and then she giggled about our animals being odd colors. "This is a yellow cow, hehehe". Sure enough, she had drawn a dark-skinned girl with black hair for herself and a white girl with blonde hair for me. We both had crowns. I was certainly not a blonde, but in comparison to her, I guess I was. We were all very touched.

And so it was that we had many adventures with humans and animals alike, *and* did our laundry. Costa Rica was wild and wonderful in so many ways - *pura vida!*

# Chapter 11: Continuing Studies

One day, dad was approached about the possibility of a family concert at the Palladium Theatre, downtown St. Petersburg. Dad had played there many years prior when it was still the Christian Science church. They had a beautiful organ, but since the church had folded it hadn't really been played. We could've easily put on a standard organ recital, with each of us taking turns on the console, but we kept toying with the idea of all playing at the same time. This, of course, required multiple keyboard instruments.

I actually can't remember which came first, the Palladium gig or 42nd Street, but around this same time all three of us accompanied the big Shorecrest production of 42nd Street. They didn't have enough money to hire a whole pit orchestra, so we volunteered the idea of accompanying the production on synthesizers, imitating orchestral instruments (but having a very obviously modern sound). It ended up being a huge success and the teenage students absolutely loved it. We spent many many tedious hours creating specific sounds on various synthesizers for a multitude of crazy effects.

So it was decided that we would do a concert of major organ works, arranged by ourselves for synthesizers. It was a big gig and it was advertised everywhere. We were in the paper, on the radio, you name it. We made flyers for the event which mom, our greatest fan, tediously handed out to every single church with which we had any connection. A gigantic (and I mean *gigantic*) poster of our faces was hung up on the columns outside the theatre. People I hadn't spoken to in years approached me and asked, "Did you know that you're on a huge poster downtown?"

Every week we packed the Suburban full of equipment and hauled it downtown to the theatre where we rehearsed. Even just the process of setting up the stage took about an hour. The show itself was a great success. It was nothing like anyone had ever seen or heard. To this day, I've never heard of anything even remotely close to what we did at the Palladium.

In attendance were a couple by the name of Norm and Lois Hannewald who were very impressed by our performance. They happened to be big figures at a local church by the name of Grace Lutheran which was currently seeking an organist/choir director. Even though dad technically got the position first, it ended up being handed down to both Jason and me throughout the next few years as dynamics changed.

Our studies in the organ were getting more and more serious. It was coming time for me to decide what I wanted to pursue in college. This was a very tough decision to make since I had so many different interests which I wanted to explore. I would've loved to continue my studies of Spanish and pursue a career as a translator or in international business. I would've also loved to have gotten a degree in English or journalism, with my strong interests in creative writing and publishing. The one study that stood out from the rest, however, was the organ. Although I had many interests I wanted to study further, music had been the only one I was absolutely sure wouldn't be a transient fascination.

I remember the day when dad and I were in the living room, discussing the various possibilities. We ultimately decided that music would be the most fulfilling and also probably the easiest with which to get a scholarship. Dad told me I could probably make it into any music program in Florida, but if I really wanted to get a scholarship, I would study this one piece he recommended. "What piece, dad?" He dug around in the cabinets by the piano and pulled out Widor's 6th Symphony. He told me that if I really wanted it, I would play that piece for my auditions. So I did.

I think the 2007 holiday season was also the first surprise visit to Chicago. You see, it was not uncommon for us to visit the big Chicago clan for the holidays, but it sometimes got expensive with all the other trips we did and activities we were involved in. Especially with the numerous church positions we held, it was sometimes impossible to escape around the Christmas season. Many years, we had to stay at home and attend the relatively anticlimactic First Night downtown St. Pete for New Year's Eve.

So on Christmas morning after all the presents had been unwrapped, we had already begun diving into our new gifts and mom was preparing lunch, dad casually walked out into the living room and announced that his printer had malfunctioned. Okay. Then dad emerged from his office carrying an envelope for each of us. We opened them, completely confused as to what was going on, and quickly realized that he had printed an entire itinerary of a trip to Chicago and we had 15 minutes to pack for it.

Dad had it planned right down to the specific music that he would start playing when we began to scramble, carelessly

throwing things into suitcases. I called up Amy and Josh and everyone, exclaiming the news, only to realize that they had known for weeks and had kept it a surprise. I don't know of any other families that have pulled this stunt.

As always, it was a grand trip to Chicago. We met up with the whole Turner bunch, exchanged gifts and stories around grandma's big round table. We goofed off with Jimmer at his work and jammed on the many keyboards at his little apartment afterward. That year, I think, was the year that he was crazy about cardboard boxes. We were probably all also sitting on cardboard boxes that time.

Naturally, we visited with the Beshoars and crashed the annual New Year's Eve party at the Eckwall's. We took a couple trips into downtown and enjoyed the hustle of the city.

Dad also set up a meeting with an organist and an opportunity to sing in his choir. His name was Dennis Northway and he was an extremely inspirational man who had completed multiple doctorate degrees despite his recurring battles with cancer. He was a phenomenal performer and composer, whose original compositions certainly pushed the boundaries of what a church choir was usually deemed capable of. For Jason and me, it gave us a whole new outlook on what a church position could actually be.

We enjoyed our little church gigs in St. Pete, but we usually didn't feel any great musical inspiration. Here was a man who was working for a church in which he really was free to do great and crazy music which was even appreciated openly by the congregation. He had stud earrings and was happy to show off his midlife crisis gift to himself - a tattoo of Bach's signature on his forearm. We were all quite taken by him.

As always, we sang to the receptionists at the Day's Inn, where we stayed year after year. We frolicked around in the snow and took lots of pictures. It was always wonderful to see the wintery landscape, which was a great contrast to Florida's endless sunny blue skies. Dad let Jason drive the rental car around a forest park and we all commented on the frozen lake. Although it was grand to see friends and relatives, we most enjoyed the times we spent, just the four of us, doing even the most mundane things.

# Chapter 12:
## Russia and the European Organ Tour

Come to think of it, a lot happened in 2008. A couple months after our trip to Chicago, I went on tour with the Madrigalians to Russia for a couple weeks. It was a grand, although bizarre, trip. The president of the college had buddies in Russia who - flattered by the fact that we had come from the USA to perform for them - basically paid for most of our meals and excursions.

After the whole ordeal of filling out documents and getting visas for the trip, in one of our orientation meetings it was casually mentioned than no one under 18 years of age could go on the trip. After being a faithful Madrigalian for years and having prepared all the music for the trip, I was devastated. Again, dad stood up for me and made some calls, exposing the situation. It was immediately remedied. I went to Russia.

Our trip lasted about 10 days in late February. We visited Moscow and St. Petersburg, in addition to a little town in remote Siberia. The trip consisted of all kinds of weird events, including meeting Russian cosmonauts, attending Swan Lake at the Bolshoi, taking the most terrifying flight of our lives in a recycled airplane from WWII, and performing on random TV shows at 3AM. But throughout most of the trip, I just wished my family was there traveling with me instead.

That summer, however, we planned another elaborate trip. This time, we decided to go back to Segovia, but not before we did some wild new travels throughout Europe.

I had formally decided to pursue organ performance in college and had been recently accepted to Stetson University on a full scholarship. Dad and I took several weekend audition trips to FIU, UF, FSU, and Stetson. My audition at Stetson was actually pretty catastrophic. I forgot to wear socks with my organ shoes that morning and halfway through my memorized Widor's 6th Symphony, in one particular section in which the pedals move in rapid octaves, one of my shoes cut into my foot rather unexpectedly and painfully. I completely blanked on the next page, yelping from the console, "Dad! Help!" The judges were kind, however, and passed it off as just a little memory slip. The rest of the audition went fine.

So with this recent decision to take our childhood studies of the organ to the next level, dad thought it might be fun to make our own organ tour of Western Europe. Dad let me plan most of it, from hostels we would stay at to churches we would visit. After a couple weeks of meandering around Europe, playing organs and goofing off, we would return to Segovia for the rest of the summer. Dad even got our exact same apartment back on the Calle Real.

Our travels started in Paris, where we visited the famous Saint Sulpice and Notre Dame. We decided not to spend too much time in Paris, though; it was crowded and expensive and touristic. We rented a car and drove northward, through the beautiful french countryside.

Our first major city was Rheims, one of the great wine capitals. We bought some of the most excellent wine for a couple measly euros and explored around the cathedral. Then we almost got locked in a parking garage. It was terrifying for about 5 minutes.

We crossed the border into Luxembourg, a tiny and fascinating country where we stayed in the town of Echternach. (4,000 pop) Our hostel was a curiously athletic place, complete with a huge rock-climbing walls and various other sporty activities. The town was adorable and that evening we stumbled upon a concert hall where their local symphony - the small town had its own symphony! - was giving a concert. We convinced the ushers to let us in for free since we were late. It was grand!

From Luxembourg we moved ever northward to Belgium and then Germany. In Cologne we visited the

Lindt chocolate factory and ate phallic sausages. We went inside the big famous cathedral, got herded around and shushed by the obnoxious clergymen who hated tourists.

The day we drove southward from Cologne it rained cats and dogs. After a few hours traveling, hungry and tired, we decided to stop in the first little town we saw off the autobahn. We ended up in Montabaur, an adorable little village nestled into the hills along the Rhein. A little street market was happening that day in the town square and we thought it might be nice to get some snacks. This was by no means a tourist location and it was extremely obvious that we were not locals. Our German was unbelievably bad and we banked on the English abilities of locals in larger cities.

A pretty, middle-aged woman who was also shopping at the market noticed our struggles and introduced herself. Her English was very good - I think her family had hosted American exchange students or something like that. Anyway, she was very kind and invited us to follow her home where she could explain on a map exactly where we were and what we could see while in the area.

Her husband was home and made us coffee. His English was also very good and he gave us a little tour of their home. They had three young children - two boys and a girl. After we told them a little about ourselves and our quest to find various organs throughout our travels, their faces lit up and they responded that their relative was a professional organist in Wiesbaden - a large city about an hour away - and could probably show us the instrument the very next day. Yes, please!

The conversations continued and we ended up spending the entire day with the Dessaur family. We went out for fancy ice creams, visited a small church in the village, and took a lovely walk up the hill to the ancient yellow castle and its surrounding gardens. The family was so unbelievably kind and welcoming. We couldn't believe that little pit stop in the rain had led to this.

Sure enough, the next day we drove to Wiesbaden with Gabriel Dessaur's number in our hands. We eventually found his church and attended the evening mass. He was indeed a phenomenal organist and played the most wild improvisations during the service. We were all blown away. Afterwards, we climbed up into the loft and introduced ourselves. He was a fun, quirky man who was just as welcoming as his brother's family. After chatting for a while and exploring the instrument, we thanked him graciously for his time. He told us to hit up Mainz the next day and visit a cathedral there, whose organist was a friend of his. I can't think of any other instrument in which there is such a unique community of musicians, eager to meet others and share their instruments.

As we left his church, still raving about his improvisations, we bumped into some familiar faces. Knowing we would be in Wiesbaden that day, the Dessaur family had spontaneously driven there to see us again. We couldn't

believe it. Naturally, we spent the rest of the evening enjoying a long dinner and great conversation. What a great thing we had stumbled upon!

The organ in Mainz was no joke, as Gabriel Dessaur assured us it wouldn't be. The instrument had 6 manuals and we clocked the cathedral acoustics at an unbelievable 12 seconds. I mean, that's just crazy. Anyway, the organist let us sit at the console and play for a bit. We had never experienced so many keyboards and such a reverberant space. It was really something.

From Mainz, we made our way ever southward to the little town of Worms where we visited the church door where Martin Luther nailed the 95 Theses and the Lutheran church really began. (The door is surprisingly very small.) Then we hit up an enchanting little town called Speyer, where I had already contacted an organist prior to our trip. After getting miserably lost again, trying to find where we were to meet him, we ducked into a little bookstore and asked if they knew of Christoff Keggenhoff. Well, of course they did. He was the town organist and we were already on his street.

Another organist, Dr. Craig Cramer, was also in town visiting Keggenhoff. We finally found Keggenhoff's door and he welcomed us in to wait for Dr. Cramer, who had just stepped out, so we could all visit the church together. We must've looked completely ridiculous all squeezed together on his little couch because as soon as Dr. Cramer opened the door, he laughed and commented that we looked like birds on a wire.

The two organists were both phenomenal musicians and fascinating people. We spent the entire afternoon dorking out about organ literature and various other instruments we had been lucky enough to play.

At the Speyer cathedral, they played a few of their favorite selections for us on the instrument first and then gave us a couple hours to play whatever we wanted. I remembered most of my Widor. I think Jason played a big Bach piece he had recently performed. It was a glorious instrument and it was great to be able to just stretch out for a couple hours and enjoy it. That evening, we all got together at a traditional German biergarten and laughed over a few drinks. The town was right on the Rhein river and filled with gorgeous parks. We strolled around and admired the sunset together.

All the while, we continued using the great German sentences we had been practicing, like "Wir sind vier" (There are four of us) or dad's favorite which was to explain how mother was a nurse, but *not* an ambulance. ("Sie ist eine Krankenschwester aber nicht einen Krankenwagen") In one of the hostels where we stayed, dad tried to formulate his epic German sentence explaining that he liked the toothpaste in Germany because it only requires a quarter turn of the cap to open it. Clearly, this was a huge linguistic feat. Anyway, as soon as he got to the word "toothpaste" (zahnpaste), the hostel attendant just dug around and gave him some. No, no, that wasn't the point! We laughed about it for days.

Anyway, we stayed for another day in Speyer to do some more sight-seeing. There was a really cool mechanical museum with tons of historic planes and cars. Jason and dad especially enjoyed it.

Our last stop before our flight to Spain was in Stuttgart where we were all looking forward to a show by the fabulous Barbara Dennerlein. We found the general vicinity of the concert venue, but for the life of us, we could not find the building itself.

We were still very early for a jazz concert, so we ducked into a little church to ask the time and practice our German. A couple of cute old ladies who sold rosaries and postcards in the little gift shop seemed approachable.

"Entschuldigung bitte, aber, ist es 5 Uhr?" (Is it 5 o'clock?)
"Ja, ja." (Yes, yes.)
"Ist es 50 Uhr?" (Is it 50 o'clock?")
"Nein, nein", they shook their heads. Okay, great; we've got the numbers down.

The jazz club, called Jazz Bix, ended up being in front of our noses the entire time. It was somewhat hidden among the other buildings in the red-light district of Stuttgart. We likened our search to that of "the big W" from one of our favorite movies. We were so relieved once we found it.

Dennerlein was fabulous, as we knew she would be. Dad bought tons of her CDs after the show and those became our soundtrack on the endless days of getting lost in our rented Peugeot along the autobahns of Germany.

The rest of the trip involved a lot of hours on the road to catch a flight from Belgium back to Spain. We drove up and out of Germany, crossing again through Luxembourg and then finally to Belgium, which was a terribly confusing country. Along the way, we got lost at every possibility. Any time we wanted to hike off the highway in search of food, we'd end up at an emu farm or something equally strange. I remember one time we just gave up finding a place to use restrooms, so we just parked by the Rhein - one of the most important historical rivers in the world - and pissed into it.

We finally got to Brussels, where our hotel was conveniently located in the middle of the red light district, among brothels and sex shops. When we asked the hostel attendant if there were restaurants in the area, he hesitantly responded, "Yes, uh, but you won't like them". The next day we took the bus into the city center and had a few of these famous waffle things everyone couldn't stop talking about. Really, they were just normal waffles but in Belgium. We laughed at our own ridiculous situations about the red light district hostel and getting lost on the highway - all the times we had to stop in remote villages and ask, "Uh... und wo ist die autobahn?" only to be told some lengthy explanatory response in a language we didn't know. All the characters we met along the way, from welcoming families to quirky organists - it was grand European tour.

VIERBURGENBELEUCHTUNG
Neckarsteinach 26.07.2008 Abf: 20.00 HD-Stadthalle

# Chapter 13:
# Spain JJ and Stetson

After our elaborate and ridiculous travels through France, Luxembourg, Germany and Belgium, we headed back to our old stomping grounds in Segovia. Valentin rented us the same duplex where we had stayed in 2004. It was surreal to return. In some ways, nothing had changed. In some ways, everything had changed.

The streets were all the same; the aqueduct had not budged. Every summer, the patron saint of Segovia - San Frutos - magically turns another page in the book of life, on the facade of the great cathedral in the town square. (There is definitely a little string connected to it.) Mom was quickly contacted by Justo and Gustavo and Julia. Dad went back to playing with Rodrigo the drummer and Parra the bassist.

I did not get back together with Manu - he was in Madrid for most of the summer, in the height of his college degree program. Gabi, Bea and I hung out but things were different now that they had serious boyfriends. Both Jason and I ended up hanging out with a different crowd than we had expected. Perhaps this was for the best; we were able to form and develop friendships with new people and share new experiences. As always, there was never a shortage of things to see and do in Segovia. With all the summer festivities and concerts and wild parties, all we had to do was step outside onto the Calle Real.

There were many nights of sipping anis at Cafe Bohemio, a bar which quickly became a second home. The calimocho botellones of El Salon and Los Zulus raged on, night after night. Sometimes, we'd go out late at night as a family just looking for drunks to talk to. We'd goof off and tell them jokes and ask them to repeat the jokes, laughing as they stumbled over their words and created ridiculous non sequiters instead.

One time I remember the local news was shooting an interview by the aqueduct, where Jason and I happened to be walking around. We made a point to walk in view of the cameras over and over again while mom, who was watching it on TV back at the duplex, laughed over the phone. Every summer there was also an elaborate weekend-long festival celebrating the full moon. (Spaniards will use any excuse to throw a party.) The city streets were very much alive in every hour of the day and night.

I became very close with a magician named Javi, who had also attended Quintanilla but we had never before spoken to each other. He was full of energy and was fun company. We spent endless nights at Bohemio, playing with cards and goofing off. He lived in La Losa and so we took a few day trips there as well. He had a very child-like energy about him, which simultaneously intrigued and frustrated me. As someone who was entering college in a month's time, I felt it was appropriate to experience that sort of childhood again with him before what I considered to be adulthood officially began. When we left, Javi made an extremely elaborate gift for me using the first card deck he had owned. It was very special.

And so it was for a month or so. We enjoyed the summer festivals and street concerts and fireworks and everything that Segovia offered. It was by no means a similar experience to our year there in 2004, but it was a wonderful, wonderful time.

That fall, I entered Stetson University's School of Music as a freshman. Jason transferred to SPC's dual-enrollment program because the TODD program wasn't working out and he needed something academically challenging. I studied with Dr. Boyd Jones, who I quickly became good friends with as well. The instrument in Elizabeth Hall will always have a special place in my heart. Stetson was the first time I really started taking organ to the next level. I was so inspired by the other music students that I began a strict regimen of waking at 5AM, so I could get into the hall to practice on the Beckerath organ (which we lovingly referred to as "Becky") before anything in the day started.

I had never felt such a response from an instrument itself when I played it. Becky was really quite the woman. Many days, I would wander back in late at night and spend hour after hour just improvising at the console when nobody was in the building. The janitors got to know me very well, very quickly.

Anyway, on one such night, I decided to record a little composition of mine I was dabbling with - mainly a result of my improvisations. I uploaded it to Youtube and sent Dr. Jones the link. He was thrilled beyond anything I could've expected and convinced me to perform it on a student recital. It was rare that freshmen even performed on a student recital during their first semester at all, much less an original composition. I was very flattered by the response and it was a great way to jumpstart my organ studies there.

Stetson had a unique student group called Poetry at an Uncouth Hour which met weekly in a little room above the cafeteria. It was there, in late September, that I met Michael Hodges. After the recitations that evening, we went for a walk and climbed the fire escape stairs onto the roof of Chaudoin, my dormitory building. It was not something we were technically allowed to do - the rooftop was a safety concern, with splintery slats of wood all weather-worn and dilapidated. I climbed up often, regardless, and enjoyed watching the sunset, ducking down when officers drove past in their dumb little golf carts.

Mike and I fell in love. We inspired each other - him a poet, me a musician - throughout the rest of the scholastic year until he graduated and moved to Seattle for his Master's.

We have kept in touch ever since them. It was a very beautiful time for both of us; to this day, I often wake up wondering what perfect strings of words must be dancing around his mind or whether his students have any idea how lucky they are.

I also joined a jazz band called The Offbeats, which was an eclectic little ensemble of contagious personalities. Theo, our frontman was a sassy and talented black kid whose improvisations ripped off the roof. He had a big voice and a bigger personality which sometimes got in the way, but usually was just very entertaining. Our drummer, Eric, was the soft-spoken one who could be a little ditzy at times. Dan, the bassist was definitely the jokester of the group. I had a really hard time respecting him during that year, actually, because Theo and I were under the stupid delusion that our band was serious and would become famous. Dan's laid-back mannerisms often bothered me.

It's odd, because within the last couple years, he has become one of my closest friends.

As always, the Horsleys celebrated Thanksgiving with our great friends, the Adams. It was wonderful to visit with Amy, who had chosen UF as her college and had decided to study material engineering. A few hours into the evening, things would always get a bit sloppy. Huey started dropping things and giggling in the corner of the conversations. Dad would break out the songbooks and Jason would plug in his bass. Amy and I would chatter about new friends and boys and classes - typical young girl stuff.

After Thanksgiving, I returned to Stetson and to my horrible roommate, Tiffany. Even her name is horrible. Anyway, she was a big sorority girl and used to go out drinking every night until some ungodly hour. When she came back drunk, she used to throw open the door and collapse onto her bed. She had this odd drunken inclination

to turn on her hair dryer and leave it on her body while she slept. (Something about the heat or the whurring sound did it for her - I don't know.) Anyway, I would sometimes stay up late too, but it was usually to finish my music theory homework. When she came in, it was up to me to turn her hair dryer off so it wouldn't cause a fire or something. One night, however, I did not wake up when she came back home and the dryer was left on all night.

When she woke, there was a water blister on her butt where the hair dryer had been blowing heat all night. As the morning progressed, in very Willy Wonka fashion, the blister just got bigger and bigger until you could see it through her pants. It eventually popped but its scar will probably always be visible on her butt. She told her naive parents that she had fallen down stairs. I would've thought it was hilarious if I didn't have to live with her. For the spring semester, I got out of Chaudoin and moved into Conrad Hall with Anjelica Corbett.

With Christmas came yet another surprise trip to Chicago in which we were given 20 minutes to pack after dad's computer malfunctioned and printed out boarding passes. It was another wonderful reunion of family and friends, most of whom were also completely oblivious to our plans. Dad did a ridiculous babbling dance on the front porch of the Turner house, climaxing with the act of dumping a bucket of salt on his head, much to everyone's horror and laughter.

New Year's Eve was always a weird night since we wanted to party but not spend exorbitant amounts of money on some lame party downtown. After many hours of searching online and getting frustrated, we just decided to hop in the car and drive downtown. As luck would have it, we stumbled upon a huge Mexican restaurant with all kinds of festivities. The crowd was almost exclusively

Mexican and we had a blast all night speaking Spanish and telling strangers about our times in Guanajuato.

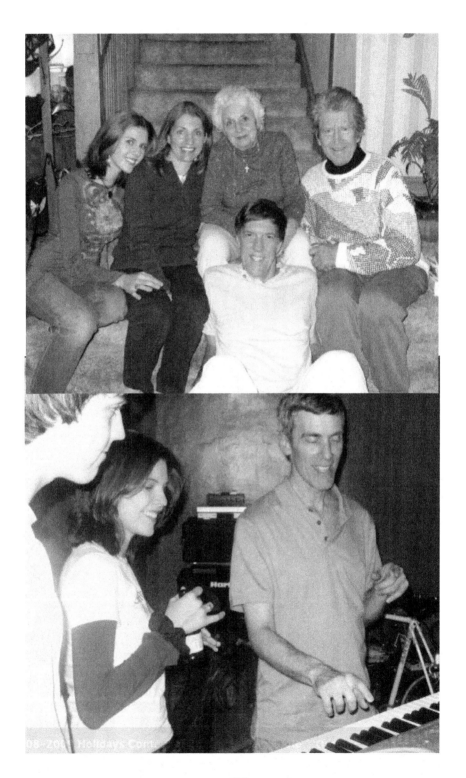

# Chapter 14:
## More Travels/Spain III

As spring approached, Spain was again on our minds. We couldn't shrug the memories of its lively streets and wild summer festivities. There was nothing in the USA that was remotely comparable to them. We had now set the bar even higher, though. We couldn't *just* go back to Segovia. We also had to include some new travels and adventures in addition to Segovia. I have no idea how mom and dad found it, but they booked us on a Mediterranean cruise boat that had not yet been built.

Cruises were not really our style. The Horsley way of traveling was far from luxurious or touristic. The cruise, however, was not your normal cruise - mainly because there wasn't a single other American on board. There was also no beginning or end to its route. People got on or got off wherever they felt like it. Its stops were in Naples, Sicily, Tunis (Tunisia), Barcelona, Marseilles, and Genoa. Pretty much all the passengers belonged to one of those places.

From our previous year's travels through Germany, we had learned how important it was to know at least a few good phrases in the foreign language. So, on the long flight across the Atlantic, we stumbled our way through a couple of Italian phrase books. While I scribbled down conjugation charts in vain, dad flipped through one of the books and promised to commit one sentence to memory. The one he learned was "Anno interroto le elettricità", which translates to, "They have shut off the electricity". We laughed and dismissed it.

We decided to stay for a week in Sorrento, a beautiful village on the west coast of Italy, before boarding the MSC Fantasia. It was an enchanting place, in many ways similar to Segovia. We had pizza with oysters on it and took long walks through the meandering cobblestone streets. We joked around with the natives and complimented them on their broken English which was far superior to the 5 words we could say in Italian. We said "grazie" a lot, which just felt weird in comparison to "gracias".

We took a day trip to hike up the volcano at Pompeii and visit the ruins of Herculaneum, which didn't look so different than the current poverty around them. We thought about the thousands of years of civilization that took place on that very ground and all the cultural developments which happened.

After one such day of sightseeing, we retired back to our little hostel in Sorrento and showered off the dust we had kicked up walking around ancient ruins. Just as we had settled into bed and had begun talking about plans for the next day, all the lights suddenly went out. As we were muttering frustrations, dad got all excited and quickly put on his robe. He ran downstairs to the reception, exclaiming with satisfaction, "Anno interroto le elettricità! Anno interroto le elettricità!" Clearly, the receptionists already knew this and were not amused.

The next few days were spent sipping limoncello and eating pizzas with oysters as toppings, topped off by long strolls by the shore. It was multiple vacations; we hadn't even started the cruise.

We hopped on the cruise at Naples, which was really a more industrial city - not like the quaint Sorrento we had enjoyed. The boat's first stop was in Sicily, but it only docked for a few hours and we were already having too much fun on the boat itself.

It was quite the study in languages, really. The vast majority of people on the boat were bilingual at the very least. Even the maids who came to make the beds every morning were fluent in multiple languages. You can't say that about your typical, even affluent American! One of the most interesting linguistic studies by far was the entertainment on board. I remember a comedy show we attended in which the comedian had to literally translate each bit into four languages. You could hear laughter erupt from various different parts of the crowd as it was translated multiple times. That was so much more entertaining than the comedy itself!

The first place we disembarked was Tunisia, a fascinating little country in northern Africa. None of us had ever been on that continent before and it was quite the culture shock. We were greeted almost immediately upon entering the port by camels. One of the camel owners encouraged us to mount the animal so he could take a picture for us.

We had heard that a good and safe way of seeing the city was to just hire a cab driver for the afternoon. That's exactly what we did. Our requests were probably a little different than those of the normal tourist. We didn't care so much for the museums or the Fodder's top-ten picks. We were fascinated by the local culture and asked to see what a typical Tunisian neighborhood looked like. It was difficult in a way to escape the consumerist tourism culture - it *was* a port city, after all.

Our cab driver took us around to various little shop-lined streets, some more touristic than others. There was one beautiful neighborhood in which every structure was painted either bright blue or white. It was a surreal sight. We stopped there to have weird tea with pine nuts in it that was supposedly authentic, although it probably wasn't and the guy just enjoyed charging us for expensive tea. Other than that, we really weren't taken advantage of, as tourists commonly are.

We didn't understand much about the political system of Tunisia at the time, but it was very odd to notice a young portrait of their leader in every store and public place. He had been in power for many, many years and it was essentially a dictatorship. He was now an older man, but it seemed like he had gotten plastic surgery to maintain appearances. At one point we happened to drive by the government palace and our cab driver suddenly got very serious. He told us explicitly to not draw out any cameras or even look for too long at the building. Security surveillance was everywhere.

When we asked to visit a mosque, the cab driver explained that men would have no trouble getting in, but mom and I would have to wear full-body hijabs. Luckily, he had a couple in his trunk and we slipped them on. It was quite the experience! Arabic architecture is, almost by necessity, unique and beautiful. Depictions of living things - animals, plants or humans - is forbidden in their art, so instead they create beautiful designs of patterns and tessellating shapes which cover the walls and the ceilings. Stunning, really. You don't find art like that very often in America.

The next stop on our route was the grand city of Barcelona. We strolled down the Rambla Principal and enjoyed the ability to actually understand the native language. It was a joy to speak Spanish again, even in the midst of the Catalan dialect. Our Castilian was perfectly understood by everyone. It was great to sit down in a bar and enjoy croquetas, patatas bravas, and tortilla espanola.

We sat by the great Dali works, munched on bocadillos and made small talk with a crazy flamenco guitarist. We even found an old music shop that had been in existence when dad played jazz piano at the casinos of Barcelona back in the 1970's. We picked up a couple scores of Spanish organ music which served us well a few weeks later when Jason and I started playing the organ at La Fuencisla in Segovia.

From Barcelona we traveled onward to Marseille where we actually did a normal tourist thing of visiting a little museum. It bragged about having an original Picasso - the one that kinda looks like an elephant - and we sat in front of it for awhile trying to appreciate it. (Not too long afterward, that same museum was robbed of that painting; I remember reading about it in the news.)

One of the most eventful stops. however, was in Genoa, Italy. Much like our adventures throughout Costa Rica, our time reached a point in which we absolutely had to do laundry. Also, like in Costa Rica, we had a really hard time finding a laundromat. I can't remember whether or not in was a Sunday or a holiday, but very few places were open and so we roamed the streets for hours, asking everybody.

As our Horsley adventures would have it, we ended up in the red light district of Genoa, hopelessly lost and burdened by backpacks full of smelly clothes. Just as we were about to give up and retreat back to the boat where we would be charged a fortune for each load, we found a helpful prostitute. She was clearly working that day - dressed in a bright pink, revealing, skin-tight dress with one bra strap over her shoulder. She told us that she was actually on her way to do laundry herself and that she could take us with her.

Sure enough, our tour guide led us on a maze around the district, ducking into alleys and taking turns left and right - we never would have found the place ourselves. Many heads were turned as we walked past sidewalk cafes and groups of people - a prostitute with an entire family behind her. I can't imagine what people must have thought.

Anyway, we finally reached the laundromat and there were plenty of machines for both of us. She tossed in her leopard-print blankets and lingerie. The five of us had a lovely conservation, laughing and cracking jokes, while we all waited for our clothes to be washed.

Our trip still wasn't over when we arrived back in Naples. We had yet to see Rome and it was only a short train ride's distance away. There we really were tourists. We saw the Colosseum, Roman Forum, Trevi Fountain, Pantheon, etc. It was amazing how much history could be found in any direction you looked. I remember one time we meandered into a church, nestled in between a few other large buildings. Around the altar was the statue of Moses by Michelangelo! The whole experience was quite a hands-on history lesson.

Once back in Segovia, again and amazingly in our old apartment, many pieces fit back together again. Dad started playing around bars, mom carted the bubushka cart back and forth from the market, Jason and I ran wild throughout the town. As we had come to expect, we could never return to the same Segovia we had left. Every time we lived there, new friendships and activities and relationships were bound to happen.

For me, I ended up getting back together with Manu for a month or so, which was really lovely. Most of the time we spent together was actually with a group of mutual friends with whom we attended rock shows, pool parties, etc.

Jason had one of his first serious relationships during this time, too. He ended up becoming very close with a beautiful girl named Marina, who was actually best friends with Javi, the guy I dated the year prior. She was a fun character with a big, lively personality which could light up the room. She had a lovely singing voice and we ended up forming a little band of sorts.

During this time, Jason was really enjoying playing the bass and he was quite proficient at it. I'm not sure how dad got him a bass during this time, but they must've either borrowed or rented a few instruments. They set up in various bars; Marina and I sang along.

Marina lived in a nearby town called La Losa and it was a hassle for her to take the train so often into town to see Jason. The two of them quickly became inseparable and she lived in the duplex with us more often than not. Jason and Marina were often perfectly content just hanging out in the apartment, having dinner and making music. The rest of us had a hard time staying inside when there was so much happening outside our door, so often they would have the place to themselves. None of us minded Marina; she was pleasant company to have around. We were all happy to see Jason enjoying someone's company so much.

It was during this trip that our good friend, Josiah, visited us. He and I knew each other from Stetson, where he was an alum. Although he graduated before I began my studies there, we had met up in various different trips to campus and a summer POE (Pipe Organ Encounter). He had never been overseas before and we invited him to spend some time in Spain with us on his first little solo tour of Europe. It had been weeks since I was in my serious practicing regimen at Stetson and I honestly missed it. I had no big summer performances to prepare for and I missed having to learn big repertoire on the beautiful Beckerath in Elizabeth Hall.

Spanish organs were historic, of course, but nothing in comparison to those of France or Germany or Stetson. They were not taken care of very well through history and, although ancient, they were not the most satisfying instruments to play. Jason and I had made connections with the nuns at La Fuencisla, a little church in the gardens downhill from the castle (Alcazar). We knew when they held masses and were welcome to walk down through the gardens and play preludes and postludes whenever we wished. It was not the greatest instrument, but it was definitely an outlet to play and that's what mattered most.

Josiah, being the academic man that he is, was fascinated by these Spanish instruments regardless of their condition and focused only on their positive musical capabilities. He showed me how to register Spanish tientos and how to deal with the flat pedal boards. It was great fun to have someone with whom I could share this. It was not easy to bring this sort of thing up casually in conversations with my friends there who wouldn't have been able to relate anyways. One of my favorite memories from his visit was our attempt to play through Bach's Dorian toccata (a piece I later used for my graduate auditions), each of us randomly taking lines with our hands or our feet as they came up, laughing all the while.

As always, it was sad to leave Manu and my friends. I could say that I was experienced now in these kinds of goodbyes, but they never really got easier. We all had a lot to anticipate though, with another busy school year on the horizon.

# Chapter 15:
## New Music and Spain IV

With each new year came new interests for all of us. Dad continued to develop LinkIt with Josh Powe, constantly learning new scripting languages and creating new capabilities for the software he had birthed. Mom was beginning to get really obsessed with health foods and organic lifestyles. Jason was now studying at SPC and enjoying professors like Dr. Cutler, who was extremely knowledgable with an entertaining teaching style. My band, The Offbeats, had broken up over some dumb wedding gig dispute that happened over the summer while I was in Spain. I was now becoming best friends with Jay who was inspiring me to get interested in music composition and the modern scene of classical music, referred to simply as "new music".

I was a bit heartbroken by the sudden resignation of one of my favorite professors, Dr. Raines, who had taken a position at Baylor instead of continuing at Stetson. My lessons with Dr. Jones, however, continued to be a motivating source which constantly drove my interest in the organ to new lengths.

Jay convinced me to take composition classes with Dr. DeMurga and attend composition forums (which were usually just composition majors) on Friday afternoons with Dr. DeMurga and Dr. Syd Hodkinson. My mind was blown by these new possibilities in modern music which I had never before been exposed to.

Jay and I quickly became an inseparable force within the music school. Within the year, we had been a part of all the New Music Machine events and premiered several original compositions on both student recitals and students composition concerts, from his three pieces for organ to Katie's crazy toy piano metal piece, to my Whirlybirds (atonal salsa piano duet) to a wild piece I wrote called Thus Spokes Zarathustra, in which Jay played the spokes of a bicycle wheel. Our audiences, even for new music concerts, did not know how to handle us.

Coincidentally, the epic student composers concert, in which we pretty much dominated the program, happened to fall on my birthday, April 16th. Being on stage with him making crazy music was the best way I could possibly fathom to celebrate.

Jay came back to St. Petersburg with me many times and each time usually resulted a big goofy jam session on weird instruments. Sometimes our friends, Nathan, Katie and Daniel, came with us. It was the best group of friends anyone could ask for; we just perpetuated ideas and silliness. I had never had so much fun making music with colleagues.

That Christmas led to another Chicago trip, this time just for dad and me. Mom and Jason decided to stay at home and hold down the house. That year, dad and I decided to go exploring some of the sights of downtown which we had yet to experience. We took in an awesome show of the Blue Man Group and we visited the Art Institute.

As always, spring came and ideas of travel were again on our minds. It was tempting to just go back to Segovia one more time and settle into whatever similar routine would follow. We reminded ourselves, however, that there was so much of the country that we had not seen at all. Spain had a huge variety of climates and cultures, from Andalucia with its flamenco and moorish influence to Barcelona with its Catalan dialect and beautiful coastal towns; in all our time there, we had not really experienced most of the country.

We always had a tendency to favor smaller towns in areas which were both topographically and culturally interesting. It was also very important that we avoid places which attract tourism; we wanted to be in Spain, not Disney.

We found a very small fishing village called Luanco, right on the remote, northern coast of Spain. It looked beautiful in the few pictures we could find and it was only a couple hours away from the larger cities of Gijon, Oviedo, and Aviles.

As always, it was hard to find an apartment for just the summer which would be comfortable for all four of us. Ultimately, we found a perfect fit. We rented a beautiful bright yellow house, about twenty feet from a dramatic coastal drop-off. The landlord even let us borrow his car during our stay.

In many ways, I was devastated that we weren't returning to Segovia. I had dreamed of getting back together with Manu and rejoining my social life there. We were all just so spoiled. It was a new adventure, though, and we liked adventures. We found ourselves once again on the front porch, with a suitcase and a backpack each, heading off to Tampa International Airport for another unknown.

Luanco was an enchanting place. The town was significantly smaller than Segovia and was significantly less touristic - there was no cathedral, castle or aqueduct. It was extremely remote and many of its inhabitants never left the town.

Naturally, one of the first things we do upon moving to another country is try to find a musical outlet. Luanco was, of course, very small and we had a hard time finding any good leads. We expanded our scope to the neighboring town of Aviles to the west and the village of Candas to the east. Sure enough, Candas (which was just a healthy walk down the shore from Luanco) had a

lovely little church whose parishioners welcomed organ students anytime during daytime hours. In Aviles we discovered a beautiful little music conservatory which housed another organ. The director told us we were

welcome to borrow the key to the office anytime we wanted to get in and practice on it. Aviles was a bus ride away, but it was much bigger than Candas and offered a lot more fun things to do.

Around this time, I had recently broken up with a guy named Chris and I was greatly looking forward to seeing Manu again even though I knew things couldn't possibly work because of the distance. He offered to visit me for a week in Luanco after his exams and then we had planned to attend a summer festival together in Galicia. It was always good to see him again, but life had affected us very differently in the past year and we had become somewhat distant emotionally. Neither of us did anything wrong, of course; we had just grown apart. It was very difficult for me to come to terms with that - I hadn't expected it - but it worked out okay in the end. We were both in very transitional and formative times in our lives and that was okay. I don't regret seeing him at all; we had lovely times together.

So we packed up and took a train to the other side of Spain on the northwest corner in a region called Galicia which was one of the remaining celtic regions of the world. Every year there was a massive celtic music festival held in a tiny little village on the coast called Ortigueira. A hundred thousand Spaniards every July would flock to this remote beach and party for 24hrs a day for an entire week. Everyone pitched tents in this campground area and we all lived without any internet, electricity, paved roads, etc. It's also important to note that the police didn't even bother making a presence. People would just post big signs in front of tents spelling out exactly what drugs they were selling and for how much. It was unbelievable.

Quiet hours were from 4-6 in the afternoon and raves went on all throughout the night. Nobody slept, ever. People walked around naked and nobody thought anything of it.

There were two faucets with running water and maybe three or four outhouses which everyone shared. It was not particularly romantic.

One memory I have from the trip which may accurately describe the mentality of the campers was one night when I was wandering through the dirt paths between tents and passed a man offering face-paintings. He was quite clearly high and overly enthusiastic about the opportunity of painting faces. I had recently dyed my hair an unbelievable shade of red and he began exclaiming how I should have him paint my face since my hair is red and he also has red paint. I reluctantly allowed him to, assuming he would draw a little sun or a heart on my cheek. To my surprise, he just covered his fingers in red paint and began to literally paint my face. Dammit, Ortiguiera! I walked to the shore and washed it off.

Exhausted and hungover, Manu and I took the endlessly long train back to Segovia. At this point, I was in a sour mood and had very mixed emotions about the whole ordeal. I just couldn't relax and enjoy the Ortigueira atmosphere like Manu and his friends could. I was thrilled at the idea of returning to Segovia, but if I couldn't relate to Manu the way I used to, how could I expect to be with my friends there?

I finally buckled and called my parents to tell them that things had turned out a little differently than I had expected. I wanted to go back to Segovia, but I needed somewhere else to stay. Jason, who said he could use a little adventure, offered to meet me in Segovia and spend a few days with me there.

Looking back on it now, it's ironic how the whole thing panned out. For months and months, all I could think about was going back to Segovia and spending time with the man I loved from years prior, Manu. In reality, I did end up going back to Segovia and spending a fabulous time with a man I loved, except that man ended up being my brother.

At first I had my doubts whether it would be enjoyable. Naturally, Jason and I had our occasional disagreements about things and we preferred vastly different lifestyles. In actuality, it was the best possible thing that could have happened. Jason and I got a room at the Don Jaime hostel - the exact same hostel where we first stayed as a family back in 2004 when we had first arrived in Segovia - and we spent every day doing whatever we felt like doing together.

I had finally grown out of my silly self-conscious tendencies of being worried what Spanish teenagers would think of me hanging out with my little brother or speaking English in public or not making drastic measures to dress or act like a native. I had nothing to prove to them or to myself about who I was or what I represented in Segovia.

Of course Jason and I were always close growing up. We played together, sang together, learned together and traveled together. We never really fought or had any period in which we distanced ourselves from each other. It seemed, however, that all those times were still cloaked in the light of childhood. Yes, we were close, but not yet as young adults. We never really talked about the deeper things that were perhaps going on in our lives or the thoughts that tugged at our minds which we felt couldn't possibly be shared.

We did everything. We trespassed through the gates of Quintanilla to walk through the empty hallways and classrooms. We walked up and down the Calle Real dozens of times, greeting the same shopkeepers and cafe owners from years past. It seemed like we were the only people in the world who ever moved.

We went back to the library and looked up dad's book in their database. We hung out in the Plaza Mayor and ate ice cream cones. We bought way too much candy from Pitoches, the same little store we used to frequent after school and before lunch. We sat on patios and drank pitchers of sangria all afternoon. We discussed philosophy and life and government and school and family and absolutely everything. There was no place we needed to be, no homework we needed to finish and no show to prepare for. It was perfect.

During our times there, we did get together once or twice with Gabi and Bea. It was a very different social dynamic now that Jason and I were in a very new Segovian mindset. It was fun to see my closest friends from high school again, but there was no pressure to necessarily re-kindle anything. Just as with Manu, I found myself feeling differently about things. Of course, I still enjoyed their company and it was wonderful    to    see them    again,    but everything was very  different than before.

It was very clear that Segovia was, for the first time, not the present. Segovia was our past. And although we embraced it and loved the city just as we always had, it felt like a playground. It was just a vessel that contained thousands of memories for us. I remember standing under the grand aqueduct which had always served as the meeting point, the place where everything happened. I looked at the boulders holding it together, amazingly just stacked on top of each other with no sort of adhesive. It was under these 2000-year-old arches that Manu and I would escape during recess to make out. It was under these arches that I would eagerly await my friends in the evenings, anticipating great nights of shows and drinking and dancing and all the other terribly cool things we did. It was under these arches that the three of us - Gabi, Jason and me - hauled up the stairs with heavy backpacks as the sun rose each day for school. A thought suddenly occurred to me that had never previously crossed my mind in the many years that I had stood at the aqueduct: *It's just a bunch of rocks.*

When Jason and I left Segovia that time, I realized that it might be a very long time before I would be back. As I looked out the train window and saw the town get smaller and smaller, I realized that everything was completely, beautifully okay.

# Chapter 16:
# Scandinavia and Leaving Spain

Of course, that summer we couldn't *just* have adventures in Spain. There were more places we had yet to experience. Dad and mom discussed the possibility of visiting Egypt - the pyramids would certainly be something to see in person. When we looked at the weather forecast for Cairo, however, with temperatures hovering around 100 degrees, we decided to look elsewhere.

We ultimately decided on a Scandinavian exploration for the last week of June. I booked the flights and coordinated the hostels as I had done with our Germany trip a few years prior. We flew into Frankfurt and then took a flight out the next day to Oslo, Norway. Of course, low-cost European airlines often came at a serious inconvenience and we quickly found ourselves in an almost comical battle with Ryanair. Since we had not printed out our boarding passes before arriving at the airport, we were told that we had to pay a ridiculous 40 euro fee to print each one. Naturally, dad wouldn't accept this and negotiated a more reasonable situation. After many demands in multiple languages, dad ended up actually behind the Ryanair counter, doing their work as an employee. All we could do was laugh.

Oslo was very curious experience. The downtown area was actually quite dirty and sketchy, especially for a Scandinavian capital. Women who were obviously prostitutes wandered the streets and there were many homeless beggars. The biggest tourist attraction was the unbelievable currency exchange. We did the math and calculated each little purchase into dollars. You want $16 for a cup of coffee? What?

We decided to get out of the capital and explore the more beautiful parts of the country. We found a train that crossed the country from Oslo on the east coast to Bergen on the west. It was a whole day-long journey through the most topographically diverse landscapes. We passed through lush green forests to pure white glaciers to dramatic, snow-covered mountains, to huge waterfalls. The fjordal villages didn't even look real from the train. We tried to imagine what it would possibly be like to live somewhere so completely remote.

I saw a young Norwegian man sitting by himself in one of the train cars and confidently assumed the seat next to him. We ended up talking throughout the entire 8-hour-long trip. I told him about Segovia and the friendship I had with my brother. I told him about Manu and Ortiguiera, my organ studies, my crazy family, etc. He told me about life in Norway and the little fjord where he grew up. Sometimes the train would stop for 20 minutes while the conductor had a smoke and we would step out into the crunchy snow, admiring the beauty of some random landscape in the middle of Norway. As his stop approached and our conversation came to an inevitable end, I told him to kiss me. I looked up at me, startled, and with his thick Norwegian accent asked, "may I?" It was an encounter that one would only expect in a movie. All I know is his name, Karl.

Before making it to the west coast, we stopped in a little village called Flom where we decided to take a boat through the fjords. As always, we talked with everyone on board. It was amazing to think that much like icebergs, as high as the mountains were above the water level, there was also probably that same amount underneath. The water was immeasurably deep.

We ended our Norwegian leg of the trip in Bergen, a fishing town on the west coast, and hopped another plane to Stockholm.

We had a very friendly taxi driver for our ride from Bergen to the airport. After some small talk and mentioning that we were all musicians, our driver mentioned that we would be passing the house of Edward Grieg on the way to the airport. He said he wasn't in a hurry that day and that he wouldn't mind if we wanted to check it out. What a thrill! Of course we wanted to check it out. We paid our driver's admission ticket and we all explored the composer's house and its adjacent museum.

From the airport, we took a taxi to our hostel. Although the taxi driver, like most Scandinavians, spoke flawless English, it seemed as though he was leading us away from any area where a hostel might be. He reassured us that he was taking us to the exact address we had given him and that he knew his way around very well. Sure enough he dropped us off on a boat dock, right on the bay. Our hotel was a boat. We fondly referred to it for the next few days as our "boat-el".

The most fascinating experience we had in Stockholm was our visit to a particular museum that was essentially a huge 7-story ship from the 1600's. The history behind it was just as fascinating as the boat itself. It was built quickly and carelessly in political haste and therefore did not undergo necessary tests before its departure. It sank on its maiden voyage, before it had even gotten out of the bay. There it sat, at the bottom of the deep water for hundreds of years until very recently when it was suddenly discovered by some scuba divers. Because of the conditions of the water in the bay, it had been beautifully preserved. Through lots of effort and funds from the Swedish government, it was then dragged to a shallower part of the bay and a museum was built around it. The mast can be seen protruding from the roof of the building. The museum was called Vasa, after the ship. We must have spent an entire day in that museum.

Come to think of it, there was a running naval theme throughout our entire Scandinavian trip. Another really interesting ship we encountered in downtown Stockholm was a docked sailboat called the Chopin, named after the composer. Basically, it was a ship for college-aged Europeans which stopped at various different ports throughout Europe. (If you connected the dots of its route on a map, it was the very very rough outline of Chopin's face.) It was free to travel on, under the expectation that everyone was crew and did work on the ship. People would take shifts all throughout the night and Chopin's music was played constantly from various speakers on board. When they docked, they brought wooden sculptures in the shape of pianos onto land as an art project. Cans of paint were available for anyone walking by to use on the pianos.

Our days in Scandinavia were grand. We spent most days roaming the endless cobblestone streets and telling jokes to natives, as we usually do.

Upon returning to Luanco, we reunited with our new friends and neighbors. We had all grown to enjoy different aspects of life there. We loved our sunset strolls along the coastal cliffs and the cool ocean breeze. The family that lived right next to us was very friendly and I often socialized with the daughter, Ana, and her friends.

One of my favorite evenings was the night we heard a piano concert in the nautical museum. The pianist, Maite, was a college student and this was serving as her degree recital. A beautiful steinway was placed in the hull of the ship which was the museum. There were fishnets hanging from the walls and the sunset splintered its way through the circular crew windows on either side of the ship walls. It was as beautiful as her performance. She played several selections by Ligeti and I was reminded of all the new music experiences I had shared with Jay and my other friends at Stetson. It was a perfect evening.

 One of the most entertaining aspects of the Asturian culture was its obsession with its local cider. Apple trees flourished in that climate and the Spaniards let many of them ferment. There was an entire culture associated with the "sidra" of this region. Every restaurant and bar served the stuff and there were tons of "sidrerias" which only sold cider.

Cider always came in a green glass bottle which was the shape of a beer bottle, but the size of a wine bottle. The bartender would then provide customers with the appropriate cider glasses, which were wide-rimmed and made from very thin glass. (They broke all the time and they didn't bother making them from quality material.) The method for consumption was to hold the cider bottle as high as possible in the air with one hand and to hold your cider glass as low as possible with your other hand. Then about a shot's worth of cider was precariously and quickly poured such that it bounced off one side of the glass and was left swirling inside the glass. It had to be drunken very quickly before it settled. Many Asturians would enjoy showing off by holding the glass behind their backs or pouring the cider from even wilder angles. The Asturians had a word for this crazy pouring process in order to aerate the cider - "escanciar." This word does not exist in English.

Naturally, the "escanciar"-ing would lead to cider all over the ground and by the end of the night, every street was riddled in a layer of sticky cider. I remember sometimes even washing my shoes off when I got home from a late night. Locals would drinks bottle after bottle of cider shots - they were about the alcohol content of beer - and some fancier restaurants even had machines which shot out shot-sized amounts of cider. The best cider came from bottles with no label. Cider coupled with the crazy seafood cuisine of gooseneck barnacles and bizarre crabs - it was quite the culture, really. But all things eventually came to an end. We left the quaint village of Luanco and headed back to Tampa International Airport.

# Chapter 17:
## The Beat of our Own Drums

The year 2011 was the year we all began to really follow our own insuppressible dreams.

After returning to Stetson and continuing my studies of German — music performance majors had to take an obligatory two semesters of a foreign language and Spanish didn't count — I found myself falling in love with the study of another language. My professor, Dr. Dysart, was very inspiring and I had become close friends with the study abroad students from Germany. I signed up and was accepted to a semester abroad in Freiburg, Germany.

Jason was being pulled in many different directions during his senior year of high school. He was in the middle of the difficult conversations which are expected at that age - questions about what career to pursue or where to go after high school. Much like his father, Jason was a trail-blazer and had his own very strong ideas about what he wanted to do which were perhaps less than socially normal and difficult to understand.

Mom and dad were restless as usual, despite our recent travels to Spain and Scandinavia. Dad needed to constantly occupy himself with new challenges in his work and was getting frustrated by some of the decisions Josh Powe was making regarding his software. Often, in the evenings, dad would break out the maps again and just start Googling small Spanish-speaking towns in various South American countries. Mom returned to the hospital, but was also burnt out in some ways by that routine. We were all stir-crazy in our own ways.

Even though we were always close as a family, it was very difficult for Jason to hold these conversations about "the future" with mom and dad. It became a nightly routine and it was difficult to make any progress regarding a good plan for either Jason or my parents. When Jason finally admitted that he had an ongoing interest in the military, mom and dad didn't know how to respond. We had always considered ourselves to be an extremely open-minded family, but that was just something we couldn't understand. Dad and Jason talked it over and over and each time Jason tried to explain himself, dad listened but couldn't really see Jason's side. And, vice versa, when dad tried to convince Jason to attend college instead, all Jason could relate to was the less than passionate crowd at St. Petersburg College and the academics there which still didn't really challenge him.

I am convinced that 99% of all human problems and suffering come from our constant attempts to express ourselves and not really being able to.

Mom and dad decided to get another dog from the humane society. It had been a few years since Dolly's death and it was weird to not have a dog around the house. Jason had also expressed an interest in having a dog. They picked up a little black lab mix which ended up being the most loving and affectionate dog in the world. Jason named him Sir Robert Boyle, after the famous 17th century French physicist.

Dad also bought a motor boat around this time. They loved taking the boat out on weekends - it was so much more enjoyable than spending too much money at the movie theaters to watch mind-numbing blockbusters. The family got into water-skiing and Robert was surprisingly okay being on the boat as well.

Although Jason and I were very close, especially after our stint together in Segovia, I was on campus at Stetson and couldn't visit home very often. Neither of us were really into long phone conversations and so we didn't get to talk much unless we were together. One day I called up Jason to ask for help with my computer, which had a virus. He drove up that afternoon - he had the

Bonneville that year - and fixed it for me. We got to chat for a couple hours and he admitted that we was torn regarding decisions about his future. It was affecting him greatly, especially mom and dad's inability to understand his interest in joining the army, and he was really quite upset about it. He felt trapped and it would have ironically been much easier if we weren't so close as a family and didn't care as much about what he chose to do.

As usual, we celebrated Thanksgiving and Christmas with our dear friends, the Adamses The evening always ended with all of us, drunk, taking weird instruments into the streets to entertain our neighbors (who clearly did not appreciate our spontaneous performances). There was a certain tension in Jason's manners, but we weren't wise enough to know how to discuss it. I'm not sure how we could've handled it better, but at the time, we often tried to dismiss it. I went back to Stetson and my friends; I assumed Jason would figure it out.

The months passed, I gave my junior recital, plans were sedimented regarding my studies abroad. I enjoyed hanging out with my closest friends on campus - Jay, Nathan, Emily, Quentin. We went to shows at DaVinci's, which was the only cool place in DeLand, and we spent endless evenings goofing off in Elizabeth Hall. Nathan, Jay and I kept performing ridiculous pieces for student recitals and drinking with our favorite professors.

As usual, we went to Chicago for Christmas to visit mom's family and dad's friends.

Since Germany is on a summer/winter semester schedule instead of our American standard of fall/spring, I had some time to kill after my fall semester at Stetson before my studies in Germany began.

Dad decided to try to teach me how to program. Every morning I pulled up an extra chair into dad's office and we scripted. I was so completely clueless, it was embarrassing. I had never really understood what dad did every day and it was quite the eye-opener. After a week, I finally made my "hello world" application and after a few weeks I had created a very simple program which could populate and organize databases. We used a scripting language called LiveCode, which originated from the whole Metacard/Hypercard/Runtime family. Although dad claimed it was "English-based" because it ran off of sentence-like commands, it seemed nothing like English to me. I mean, I considered myself good at learning languages, but this was nothing like I had ever seen. Among many other things, I had a new level of respect for my father's profession.

I booked my flight for Germany for the last day of February even though my semester didn't start until April. I told mom and dad that I had contacted numerous organists in various cities of Germany and that I would be traveling to meet them in the month before my classes began. This was somewhat true; I had contacted organists and I did have ideas about where I should go, but I ultimately and intentionally arrived in Germany with no idea what I would do the next day.

 It was invigorating, really. I had never traveled alone like this before and I pretty much let the wind decide my journey. I traveled for 33 days. I could say that it was alone, but that is also not really true. I talked with everyone. After a few days, I came to the realization that I could do whatever I wanted to do and be whoever I wanted to be. I didn't know anybody and nobody knew me. I began to act accordingly. It was an extremely liberating feeling.

On the steps of the cathedral in Cologne, I held up a sign stating, in German, that I would speak to anybody about anything. I just wanted to practice my German. That weekend was the Karnaval, the German equivalent of Mardi Gras, and the streets were filled with people. Tons of folks, from business men getting off work to totally drunken party-goers, approached me to tell me jokes or to flirt or to share ideas they had.

I played all sorts of social games. I enjoyed meeting people on trains and making a point of not saying anything that was remotely true, just to see how long I could keep it up. People had no reason to doubt my honesty. I had nothing to prove other than my freedom to myself.

I also really enjoyed asking strangers really personal things. I liked asking for secrets and when people hesitated, I simply convinced them that I would probably never see them again and that it was therefore safe. Some of the secrets I collected were really trivial and funny, others were dark and serious. I wrote them down in my little moleskin notebooks which I brought with me everywhere.

In Dusseldorf, I couchsurfed with an animator and drank traditional Killepitch. In Heidelberg, I stayed with Jon, an American who spoke flawless German and whose stories were the most inspiring things I had heard in a long time. We drank pickled peach juice and he told me about his own wild, unconventional travels. I spent a scary night in the train station of Hannover on my way to Leipzig because I absolutely had to attend Sunday services in Bach's churches. I experimented with a carpooling service called mitfahrgelegenheit and had lovely experiences traveling with strangers, pitching in for gas. I walked the underground catacombs of Prague and drank absinthe which, by the way, is totally gross. In Berlin, I couchsurfed with a incredibly fascinating man named Puneet, who gave speeches for TED talks and had no concept of possessions. I visited the museums and went to one of the greatest secrets of Berlin - the Salon zur Wilden Renate - a bar which had an entire alternative reality created by mad artists behind one of its doors. I became very close friends with a German mathematician named Daniel Renz and within an hour of talking, I invited him to spend a few days with me in Copenhagen at the end of the month.

I met a Fulbright composer named Jason in Hamburg and we fell madly in love within a day after stumbling into anti-nuclear protests and spectacular carnivals. I turned pages for a very eccentric and friendly organist in Bremen and then was platonically offered a room in the apartment of my hostel attendant, after spending many hours chatting with him. I met another composer in Copenhagen and sat in on an unbelievable rehearsal at the conservatory. I chatted with prostitutes and we had a pretty ridiculous evening involving the consumption of space cakes.

I had an almost disastrous evening in Flensburg on my way to Copenhagen in which I almost didn't find a place to stay, but then finally stumbled upon a vending machine hotel. (Those exist, apparently.) In Copenhagen, Daniel and I explored the harbors and the interesting socio-political experiment of Christianya, a section of the city in which there was no law and drugs were sold openly. From Copenhagen, I went back to Bremen and then booked a cheap flight out the very next day to London because why the hell not.

In London, I attended a little punk show and met a woman who said I could call her Barbara but it wasn't her real name. We had one completely wild night of bar-hopping and dancing at discotheques and hailing a cab at 4am to her flat which was an hour or so north of the city. She was squatting in an illegal apartment and we

crashed hard. I missed my flight that morning and ended up with an extra day in London, a day I was not supposed to have.

I wandered the streets and it didn't feel real. Nothing could have possibly been real about that day. The 32 days of untamed adventure had changed me in ways I could never have expected. I couldn't believe that it had all actually happened and I was still alive.

I walked aimlessly up and down the river, trying to absorb all the things that had happened and all the people I had met. Magically, as if I was in a movie - I often thought I was - I stumbled upon a street poet. He had a little lantern on the ground which illuminated his corner of the street which he had covered in brightly colored letters, each titled and containing a poem. He offered to recite or give poems.

I approached the old man and we talked for a while. He refused to say much about himself and so I told him briefly of my adventures. I have no idea how long we talked - the streets were rather empty at this point. He had the most poignant, short responses and a certain brilliance in his wrinkly eyes. As the conversation came to an end, he told me that he had the perfect poem for me. He dug around his pile on the ground and pulled out a bright blue envelope titled, "The Journey". I gave him whatever change was in my pockets, which was now currencies of multiple countries - I have no idea how much it amounted to.

For whatever reason, I doubted the poet was actually that much of an artist. He was on the streets, after all. I sat on a bench overlooking the river, opened his envelope, and wept. It was perfect. It was more than perfect. He had even quoted some of its lines in our conversation - how did he do that? I ran back to the place I met him, but he was gone. The next morning, I boarded my flight back to Germany and that concluded my epic 33 days of solo travels.

The Paedagogische Hochschule in Freiburg was a wonderful experience. I refused to socialize with other international students and I signed up only for classes taught in German for German students. I practically lived in the little music school and got involved in everything I could. I played piano for their Big Band, took both piano and organ lessons, sang in the college choir, accompanied their orchestra - I even found an elite new music group which specialized in the music of John Cage. We held long rehearsals for weeks and weeks and finally gave the most ridiculous performance of my life in an art gallery. I even composed a piece for the program.

I biked everywhere and I don't remember a single day I was home before midnight. I spent hours upon endless hours in the KuCa, a pay-what-you-can coffee shop by the music building. I became best friends with Alex Schuler, a wonderful guy who introduced me to so many other wonderful people. I also spent a lot of time with Stefan Dautel, who studied at Stetson the year prior. I had a phenomenal social life, unlike anything I ever had at Stetson. I became fluent in German and even had some traveling within my semester, which included a spontaneous trip to Eastern Europe which I should also probably mention.

I booked a flight from Germany to Thessaloniki and then a return flight from Istanbul back to Germany, assuming I would find a way of getting there. I did, and my travels involved more wild couchsurfing stories. Stelios, a Sicilian sitar-player hosted me in Greece. I saw his band  perform that night in an abandoned schoolhouse on the beach and when the neighbors began throwing raw eggs onto the stage from their balconies in complaints about the noise level, the band just played on.

I took a terrifying bus ride through Macedonia and into Sofia, Bulgaria where I stayed at a ridiculously cheap hostel until I attended a little theatre show at the local university where I met Deniz Serifoglu, who invited me to save

money and stay with her for a few days. Everything was incredibly cheap for me since the Bulgarian currency was so weak against the euro and their economy never really recovered from its history under the oppressive Soviet control. A night out, complete with fancy dinner, a show, etc. cost me the equivalent of about $4. It was easy to splurge on Deniz. She had a fascinating life story and it was an honor to get to know her. During my time in Sofia, I also stumbled into a thousand-year-old church, tucked under a highway, where I met Erling Wold and his wife. Erling was a composer at Berkeley and was in Sofia for the premiere of his requiem, which he gave me a copy of. It was a very inspiring little encounter and I fell in love with the requiem. It became the soundtrack for my Eastern European travels.

As anticipated, I ended up in Istanbul couchsurfing with a man named Ahmed. As a child, when asked what I would want to see in the world, I always answered the Hagia Sofia, mainly because it seemed so impossibly faraway. I never imagined I would ever make it that far across the

world. Sure enough, I found myself inside the Hagia Sofia and watching whirling dervishes in Istanbul, in the bridge between Europe and Asia. It was in Turkey of all places that I bought a little purple ukulele which I found in a little corner shop. It became something quite dear to me, actually; everyone should have a cheap, portable instrument because they will never hesitate to bring it everywhere they go.

There are so, so many stories I could share here but this book is not about me. Those stories are also better suited for late-night conversations around the pool deck and bottles of wine.

It was in May that I got the infamous phone call from Jason. I was on my way to catch a train to Zurich to see a Schoenberg opera there. His voice seemed so low. I wondered, was his voice always this low? He told me that he had decided to join the army and that he was leaving to attend boot camp. I asked when. He said tomorrow. I asked if mom and dad knew. He said he had just told them. I asked him if this was what he really wanted to do. He said yes. I told him that I was so sorry for ever criticizing his ideas of joining the army. I felt like I had not been supportive of him, as I should have been, as he always had been for me. He told me not to worry about it and that he would write me letters when he could. I told him I loved him and he told me he loved me back. The conversation was short. For the rest of the day, I couldn't feel my body. Nothing seemed real.

For the next few weeks, I got phone calls from mom and dad every day. Jason was gone and we kept trying to put the pieces together. Sometimes mom and dad would have to keep passing the phone back and forth because they'd start crying and wouldn't be able to speak. I sat by the Dreisam river and wondered what Jason was feeling or looking at or eating or thinking. We were always so close as a family; why weren't we better at talking about this while he was still home? He turned things over and over in our minds, but had no answers.

As the months passed, it became very painful for mom and dad to stay at home during the summer without Jason there. They decided to take a couple trips, hoping to relax a little and take their minds off the constant worries of how Jason was doing. They chose to return to Mexico for a stint and revisited Guanajuato, just the two of them. They also took a trip up to North Carolina and reunited with an organist friend of ours there who we had known from Florida. They were considering possible retirement ideas, but nothing really stuck yet.

As the summer came and past, we began to finally accept Jason's choice and the troubles leading up to it. He and I were both at a point in which we were making big decisions for ourselves and it was just a shame it couldn't have been a smoother transition. Mom and dad were also now in the process of planning their own big decisions regarding possible retirement plans. Someone once told me that we're all going to do what we're going to do, so we should do it already. I often wonder how much of what we're going to do we have really already done.

It has only recently become clear to me that each one of us is a completely different person. We each see the world in different ways and are driven by very different fuel. It's a beautiful thing, really, that people can grow up together with many of the same experiences and yet still be affected in their own ways, becoming their own unique person. I wonder how much of us has simply always been us, waiting for a chance to speak.

In many ways, we were relieved when the army idea didn't work out. Jason wanted to pursue a very specific field but, in the midst of Obama's cutbacks, he was told he'd have to choose something else. Jason didn't accept second best and returned home after 2 entire rounds of bootcamp. I picked him up from the airport; 1 had never been so happy to see him.

So much happened in the year following. Jason became unhappy staying in Florida as any of us in his position would've been. Our dear friends from childhood, the Terrys, were now pursuing their own various interests and the eldest son, Eli, offered Jason a position in Texas. The location intrigued him, as he had always wanted to see

Texas, and he was anxious to have some camaraderie, which he didn't really have in Florida. Jason picked up and moved to Austin, Texas.

I was also hooked on the idea of starting my own career and getting out of Florida. I went through with the long and tedious process of graduate school application. I narrowed down my search and auditioned at Peabody Conservatory, Manhattan School of Music, Cincinnati Conservatory and Duquesne University. As so many young and sometimes naive girls my age, I had my heart set on NYC for a while. I had recently became very good friends with Seth, a musician from Brooklyn. I hosted him when he played shows in Deland and St. Pete; he hosted me when I auditioned in Manhattan. It was really quite a thrill to travel solo again and perform for these schools.

I ultimately had to reason with reality; I was accepted everywhere, but with vastly different financial packages. Manhattan offered me everything, but ended up giving me nothing. On the other hand, I had really connected with the professor at Duquesne in my audition. She was so much more welcoming than any other I had met in my auditions - she even picked me up from the airport and hosted me at her house! I was really quite touched by her interest in her students and her overwhelming kindness. In addition, Pittsburgh was a very affordable city and I was offered an assistantship which would cover all my tuition. I would have been a fool not to accept it.

I finished out my last year at Stetson by continuing to play harpsichord with the chamber orchestra, giving my senior recital, and visiting home as often as I could. Over Labor Day weekend, mom and dad took a weekend boating trip in Mount Dora, only about 40 minutes away from campus. It was a thrill for me to visit them there and introduce them to Alex, my good friend from Freiburg who was now doing his study abroad at Stetson. The very next day, after returning to campus, I woke up and just wanted to spend more time with them. At 7AM, I packed another over-night bag and drove back. Mom and dad never used cell phones and were still in bed when I arrived. I may have startled them a bit.

Mom was now completely invested in alternative health. She took dad to farmer's markets all the time and went out of her way to help educate people about the toxic levels in non-organic food, plastic bottles, microwaves, etc.

Dad got a fascinating gig playing organ for the Tampa Bay Lightning, an NHL hockey team. Some donor had recently given tons of money for the stadium to buy a massive theatre organ. Technically, it was the largest theatre organ in the world. They called Stetson's School of Music to find someone to play it. Dr. Jones asked me if my dad might be interested and after one interview, dad got the job.

The gig was absurd, really. We had played this instrument throughout our entire lives and still hadn't experienced the extent of its diversity. Before each game, the stadium would dramatically turn off all the lights, fire up humongous and real tesla coils, and put all cameras on dad while he performed some showy movie soundtrack or something - essentially a battle call for the game which followed. He had a crowd of 20,000 screaming fans. Dad even had his own bar directly under the console, aptly called *Between the Pipes.* The whole thing was just ridiculous.

And, as always, we celebrated the holidays with our closest friends.

Mom had finally found her calling in health sciences, with her new infatuation with organic food and alternative health. Dad had found an outlet to play organ which was not a church and was thoroughly enjoying the drastic change of scenery from church pews to raucous stadiums. Jason was living with his close friend, Eli Terry, and for the first time, living his own completely independent life. I had accepted a graduate program at Duquesne and was planning my move to Pittsburgh as soon as I graduated Stetson. Mom and dad came to Deland, Florida for the last time and helped me say goodbye to my dearest friends and professors who had changed my life.

A few days after I graduated, I packed everything I owned into old Lucille and drove by myself to Pittsburgh, Pennsylvania. I stopped in Savannah on the way and remembered that time so long ago when the strange old woman paid for our family's dinner. I stopped in a little town in rural South Carolina and joked around with the natives, remembering how many times we had done that as a family in foreign countries. I sat for a few hours at a rest stop in the middle of the Appalachian mountains and watched the sunrise while reading chapters in dad's book about our time in Segovia. I kept the book in the passenger seat through the entire trip. Was this really it? Our childhood was certainly over and this had to be the most definitive end to our times together growing up. I just couldn't believe it. All of those shows we did as Two Bees and a Honey, our street performances and late nights in Ybor City, our spontaneous trips to Chicago, our cultural immersions all over the world, our wild European adventures - I just couldn't believe that all of that actually happened. But it did happen. All of that actually happened.

# Epilogue

Where are we now? Well, Jason decided he'd rather pursue his life-long interest in video-game creation rather than hardware manufacturing and is therefore back in Florida, learning how to write software. He and his girlfriend, Cristina, now share a cute little apartment together and Robert travels from their place to home every other day. Cristina is a lovely woman and they seem very happy together. I recently got to visit them a few weeks ago.

Mom and dad have recently decided that they'll spend their retirement on adventurous travels rather than Floridian sentience and have therefore chosen to clean out the house in preparation for total mobility. They've picked out a beautiful little city in northern Argentina called Mendoza and are considering settling there after traveling around the world for a few years.

I'm beginning my second year of my Master's at Duquesne University where I'm studying with Dr. Ann Labounsky and also serving as the organ department's graduate assistant. After a year in my first music director position at a small presbyterian church in Plum, I am now working at a lutheran church called St. John's. I'm currently making preparations for directing the choirs there. In the past year, I also was in a rock band called New Shouts and we played all around town together. I'm very involved in the cycling community here and I also volunteer regularly at the Humane Society walking shelter dogs in my spare time.

It is raining as I write this, much like it often does here in Pittsburgh, and I can't help but remember the thousands of times I watched the rain fall on the little statue outside my bedroom window. Cars are passing by on the street beneath me, scraping the wet pavement and kicking up puddles along the curb. I wonder if the people in those cars have ever heard of Segovia.

This book began as an email I would've sent my father back in December on a day when I was particularly nostalgic. I wrote a few reminiscing paragraphs about our times living together. As I read the email back to myself, I kept thinking of things I had forgotten to mention. Memories started coming in whirls, in waves, in so many rainstorms and in odd moments when I was at work or in class. The past year has been the first in which all of us are apart, indefinitely. Jason and I are beginning our own lives and our own careers. Mom and dad are leaving the house we grew up in to pursue adventures without us.

I catch myself all the time doing little things which remind me of home. Just the other day, I found those stupid Wyndom Hill sampler albums that dad used to play during meals. I listened to one on Spotify while I ate dinner alone. (I *hated* those Wyndom Hill sampler albums.)

I have finished this book, fighting through such sweet tears. It has been a wild and impossibly wonderful ride. The thought keeps repeating itself over and over in my mind - *I can't believe it's over, I can't believe it's all over.* Is anything really over? We're starting our own chapters in our own books. Who's to say what adventures the future will bring? All I know for sure is what we've done in the past. We are the Horsleys and we are the luckiest family in the world. Mom, dad, Jason - I love you so much. Thank you.

*August 28, 2013*

CPSIA information can be obtained
at www.ICGtesting.com
Printed in the USA
BVOW07*1104111216
470475BV00001B/1/P